INVEST IN LIVING

G000146778

HOME~BAKED BREADS & SCONES

by

BABS HONEY

EP Publishing Limited
1977

The *Invest in Living* Series

About the Author

Babs Honey is a busy farmer's wife from Wales who has for years been doing most of the baking for her large family of husband, seven sons and a daughter. She has no time to spare for anything but a sensible, down-to-earth approach to baking, and her qualifications for writing this book are simple—she says that if she can make bread, anyone can!

Acknowledgements

The author would like to thank the many local friends who have given recipes and encouragement, and in particular Mrs. Marguerite Price and Mrs. Sarah Griffiths, without whose help this book could never have been finished. She would also like to thank her family for putting up with her experiments over the years!

Cover photograph by Studio Jon, Fishguard. Shown are Mrs Griffiths Brown Bread, Olive's Caerfarchell Teacakes, Edna's Maltless Malt Loaf and Marguerite's Griddle Scones and Potato Scones

Illustrations on pp. 8 and 9 from Mary Evans Picture Library

The publishers would like to thank Elaine Hemming, Gateware Products Ltd., Allinsons Ltd. and RHM Foods Ltd. for their assistance

Contents

Note on Metrication

Many of the recipes in this book are hundreds of years old and have been adapted by successive generations to round imperial measures of pints, ounces and so on. Rather than distort these amounts by converting them to metric measure in the recipes themselves (and also to avoid cluttering the recipes with figures of both standards) we give here tables showing equivalents which can be used when necessary.

oz	g		lb	kg		pints	litres
$\frac{1}{4}$	7		1	0.5		$\frac{1}{4}$ (5 fl oz)	0.1 (142 ml)
$\frac{1}{2}$	14		2	0.9		$\frac{1}{2}$ (10 fl oz)	0.3 (284 ml)
$\frac{3}{4}$	21		3	1.4		$\frac{3}{4}$ (15 fl oz)	0.4 (426 ml)
1	28		4	1.8		1 (20 fl oz)	0.6 (568 ml)
2	57		5	2.3		2	1.1
3	85		6	2.7		3	1.7
4	113		7	3.2		4	2.3
5	142		8	3.6		5	2.8
6	170		9	4.1		6	3.4
7	198		10	4.5		7	4.0
8	227					8 (1 gallon)	4.6
9	255						
10	283						
11	312						
12	340						
13	369						
14	397						
15	425						
16	454						

1000 millilitres (ml) = 1 litre (l)

1000 grammes (g) = 1 kilogram (kg)

Each of the recipes in this book has been given a symbol so that you can see at a glance how rich it is.

No eggs

1 egg

2 eggs

3 eggs or more

Introduction

'Give us this day our daily bread'

Every day, for thousands of years, somewhere on the earth's surface, bread has been baked. In recent years the process has become more and more mechanised, and there was a period when home-baking went out of fashion because there were so many good private bakers in business, each competing to supply bread as cheaply as possible. During this time a mystique grew up about making bread which made it appear quite beyond most people's comprehension. Now, however, the wheel has turned full circle and there are many thousands of people busy baking their daily bread and proving that it really is easy.

Bread doesn't just come in one form—there are literally hundreds of variations on the basic yeasted recipe, and an enormous number of delicious unyeasted breads too. You are probably already familiar with scone-making, and scones after all are a form of bread. Maybe you usually make just plain or fruit scones, though—how about trying griddle scones, date scones, cheese scones, bacon muffins . . .?

So why not join the army of home-bakers who prefer good wholesome home-made bread and scones to the multi-manufacturers' version? Imagine your kitchen filled with the appetising aroma of baking bread, and your family eating delicious loaves baked just as crusty as you like them . . . Well, why not? Maybe you are still suffering from some of the misapprehensions lingering from the past —for instance:

'You have to knead the dough for hours'
It's true that in Victorian times housewives thought that bread couldn't be kneaded too much. Times have changed, however, and few of us have very much time to spare today. Experience will show that kneading takes, literally, only a matter of minutes.

'I'll never be able to keep the dough warm enough'
The only difference between making bread in a warm atmosphere and in a cooler one is that in the latter, the process will take longer. If the kitchen is warm enough for you to work in, it's safe to assume that it'll be warm enough for the dough.

"Yeast is so complicated. My bread will never rise in the oven—even my cakes often sink'
The workings of yeast are explained on p. 45, but if you just remember that yeast is a living thing which can be killed by too much heat or too much salt, you won't go far wrong. By the time the bread goes into the oven all the rising is done, and the yeast will be killed by the oven heat. The process is quite different from that involved in cooking cakes, where the cake rises as it is cooked.

This book is divided into three sections dealing in turn with scones, unyeasted breads and yeasted breads. In each section, the plain, sweet and savoury recipes are grouped together and then sub-divided according to whether you will need no eggs, one egg, two eggs, three or four.

The Scone

Bread-making is one of the easiest kinds of cooking, and the scone—or biscuit, as the Americans call it—is the most simple of all. This book starts with scones, in the hope that in making this most simple form of bread, even the most nervous novices will gain confidence, and thus be encouraged to try other forms of bread-making. The wish is that the recipes included will also add variety for the advanced student of cookery, since the recipes in each section have been passed on by women from kitchens all over the world. They are offered to you as a basis for your own inspired experiments.

Any recipe, after all, is translated differently by each and every one of us in a completely unique and personal way, so don't feel afraid to try variations to suit your own 'customers'.

Unyeasted Breads

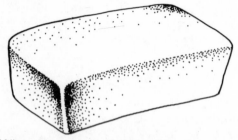

When it comes to unyeasted breads, what a feast of variety we find! It seems that nothing available has not been tried over the generations in these delicious loaves. Again, the recipes are international in flavour though, naturally, they come mainly from the western world, since rice is the staple food of the eastern countries. If anything, unyeasted breads are even more simple to make than scones, since they require no rolling out, but of course they are not as quickly and conveniently cooked.

Yeasted Breads

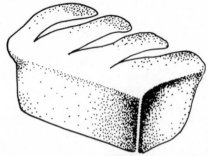

'Proper' bread-making with yeast is a creative art, it is great fun, and it gives much pleasure to others—after all, how many make bread just for themselves? Anyone can make bread, if they will—it is nearly as easy as making mud-pies. Just a bowl or board and your hands plus the simplest ingredients, and you're away. Any heater from an oven to an open fire will cook your bread (we often forget that the modern marvels of electric, gas, or even solid fuel cookers are of comparatively recent origin, and our grandmothers managed perfectly well without them). What's more, kneading the dough works off frustrations, and induces a sweet temper and a satisfied soul—and thus a happy household.

The recipes in this book are collected for your interest—may they give you many hours of happy cooking, and much joy in the eating!

Oven Temperatures

Note

This table is only a guide. Different makes of cooker vary. If you are in any doubt about the setting of your oven, it is best to refer to the manufacturer's temperature chart.

			Gas Mark					Gas Mark
Very cool	250°F	121°C	$\frac{1}{4}$	Fairly hot	375°F	191°C	5
	275°F	135°C	$\frac{1}{2}$		400°F	204°C	6
Cool	300°F	149°C	1, 2	Hot	425°F	218°C	7
Warm	325°F	163°C	3	Very hot	450°F	232°C	8
Moderate	350°F	177°C	4		475°F	246°C	9

Handy Measures

1 oz flour	= 1 rounded tablespoonful
$\frac{1}{2}$ oz flour	= 1 level tablespoon
1 oz sugar	= 1 level tablespoon
1 oz jam	= 1 level dessertspoon (pudding spoon)
4 oz flour	= 1 teacupful
8 oz sugar	= 1 teacupful
3 oz grated cheese	= 1 teacupful
2 oz breadcrumbs	= 1 teacupful
1 oz coffee	= 2 rounded tablespoonsful
1 oz dried yeast	= 2 level tablespoons or 8 level teaspoons
(Note: 1 oz dried yeast	= 2 oz fresh baker's yeast)
$\frac{1}{2}$ pint liquid	= 1 average coffee mugful
$\frac{1}{4}$ pint or 1 gill	= 1 small teacupful
1 tablespoon liquid	= $\frac{1}{2}$ fluid oz
1 pint liquid	= 20 fluid oz

* To test the capacity of your coffee mug, simply measure 2 mugsful of cold water into a pint milk bottle. They should exactly fill it.

* To test your teacup, 4 cupsful should fill a pint milk bottle.

* Roughly speaking, the average teaspoon filled twice equals 1 dessertspoon, and 2 dessertspoonsful equal 1 tablespoon.

* To save washing up, first measure out the dry ingredients and then use the same cups, spoons or jugs for the liquids. This will also keep the proportions in the recipe correct.

* To measure a level spoonful, do as the mothers do when measuring baby milk powder— fill the spoon and then level it off with the back of a knife. For half a level spoonful, simply divide lengthways with a small knife.

Easy Ways to Measure Honey or Syrup

One way is to place the tin or jar on the scales before taking a warmed spoon to dip into the honey, syrup or black treacle; the correct weight can then be taken.

If you dip a dry spoon into flour, shake off the surplus, then dip it into the syrup, the syrup will come easily and cleanly away from the spoon.

If the honey or syrup is to be melted with milk or other liquids, leave the spoon in the mixture until all the syrup, etc. has dissolved.

The Story of Flour

There was a jolly miller once,
Lived on the river Dee,
He worked and sang from morn till night,
No lark more blythe than he.

And this the burthen of his song,
Forever used to be,
I care for nobody, no, not I,
If nobody cares for me.

Traditional song from the poem by Isaac Bickerstaffe, c. 1761

Certainly that Jolly Miller had something to sing about, for he was a key man in the society of those days. No community could get on without its local miller.

Many aeons ago, when primitive men started eating the seed heads of grasses to augment their diet, they little realised what they were starting. Later, about 75,000 years ago, Man went on to pounding the seeds into a rough type of flour and gradually, as intellect dawned, the more progressive ones started clearing land and cultivating those grasses. Then, when fire was discovered the more enterprising must have thought of mixing this rough meal with water and baking it on a hot stone, a 'bakestone'.

From these early 'cakes' of bread, cooked on bakestones or on an open fire or simply in the heat of the sun, have evolved all the sophisticated forms of bread we now know—including the sweet breads or cakes, as we now call them.

Among many other commodities, we take flour—especially wheat flour—so very much for granted these days that we tend to forget the history which has gone into the production of our familiar, almost despised, daily bread. Those of us fortunate enough to be living in the affluent countries of the world have less incentive to remember much about bread, except that, we are repeatedly told, it is fattening.

Milling

In the year 2,000 BC, when Abraham was born, in Ur of the Chaldees, every Chaldean household had a courtyard containing stones for grinding the corn, and an oven. But it was the Romans, 2,000 years later, who first perfected the rotary motion with circular stones, one stationary and the other moving round to crush the grains; thus the first milling 'machine' was in production. The moving stone was rotated by slaves or animals.

In parts of rural Britain there are mills mentioned in the Domesday Book. Along the valleys of the fast-flowing rivers of the western coasts of the British Isles, mills are dotted at fairly frequent intervals, and in the Eastern counties remnants of ancient windmills are still to be found. Windmill Hill, Mill Road or Mill Street are common names in English towns and villages, demonstrating the importance of mills in medieval Britain; think, too, of the relative commonness of the surname Mills or Miller. It seems, therefore, somewhat ironical that now, when milling, like farming, has become so highly mechanised, many people are clamouring to have their oats, wheat and barley produced with old-fashioned farming techniques and to have it milled in the old water or windmills, ground with stones instead of modern rollers. Many old mills are now re-opening in consequence of this demand.

A fourteenth century woodcut

Varieties of Flour

Mrs. Beeton, who wrote her famous book on Household Management in 1857–61, had very decided views on milling flours. She was a great believer in buying wholemeal flour and eating really nutritious bread made, preferably at home, from wholemeal flour. 'The whiter the bread, the less nourishment it contains', she declares, and to prove her point quotes the story of Majendie, who fed a dog for forty days with white bread, at the end of which time it died; while another dog, fed on 'brown' bread made with white flour mixed with bran (customarily called brown bread in those days, it seems), 'lived without any disturbance to its health'.

In America, too, in the early part of the nineteenth century a Dr. Graham was putting forth theories, which today are accepted by many dietetic authorities, that valuable nutrients are lost when any fraction of the grain is removed and that the resulting products lack important vital elements.

Dr. Graham found a vigorous supporter and protagonist in Britain in the late Mr. T. R. Allinson who, in 1895, founded the firm of Allinsons, which has been dedicated ever since to the proposition that bread should be made of 'wheat, the whole wheat and nothing but the wheat', stoneground under conditions of maximum purity.

Since many of us are home bakers of bread because we *prefer* our own tasty efforts to the 'cotton wool' pre-wrapped-untouched-by-human-hand type of bread which can be seen in all kinds of shops these days, it stands to reason that we are going to want the best flour it is possible to buy. There can be little doubt that the best flour is indeed wholemeal flour, as advocated by Drs. Graham and Allinson, and if a preference is felt for flour made from wheat grown on the compost system (i.e. from 'naturally' grown wheat using no artificial fertiliser), then you only have to shop around in health-food shops or the more specialist grocers' shops.

Some fortunate souls may live near one of the newly-opened mills. The county libraries usually carry special knowledge of this nature, so if you require locally milled flour, make enquiries.

However, it may be that, owing to dietary requirements, wholemeal flour is too 'rough', or you may wish to experiment with recipes using white flour. Then you will require different flours for different types of cooking.

Facts about Flour

We use mainly flour milled from wheat, though it can be made from potatoes, rice, maize and all cereals. Oatmeal, of course, is used in Scotland in such national dishes as porridge, and that vital part of every Burns' Night supper, the haggis. Flour can even be made from bananas! However, the common factor in all ordinary flours is gluten, an elastic substance formed by the addition of water to flour proteins. Gluten is capable of being stretched or 'blown up' by bubbles of gas produced during fermentation or by the action of heat on baking powder (and other raising agents), forming the framework of the finished loaf or cake.

Barley is low in gluten, but peasants in Europe used to rely on it as it grew better than wheat in Northern latitudes. During the Second World War we could supplement our diet with barley flour, but it is much heavier than wheat flour.

Rye is also grown in Northern climates where wheat does not grow well. Rye flour usually consists of the whole substance of grain and is therefore richer in protein than white flour.

Different Types of Flour

Flour is often classified in terms of extraction rate, i.e. the percentage of the whole grain that remains in the flour after it has been milled.

From left to right: rye, wheat, barley, oats and hard wheat

Wholemeal flour has an extraction rate of 100 per cent because it must contain the whole of the cleaned wheat.

Wheatmeal flour has some of the coarsest bran removed; the extraction rate is 85–95 per cent.

Both these flours may be plain or self-raising, coarsely or more finely ground, stoneground and compost-grown.

Because both contain all or a high proportion of bran and germ, baked goods made from them rise less and have a closer texture than those made with white flour.

General purpose flour usually has a 70–72 per cent extraction rate.

Self-raising flour is suitable for general household use and many housewives use it exclusively. It is popular because it eliminates errors in calculating exact amounts of raising ingredients for any particular recipe, and ensures that the raising ingredients are evenly blended throughout the flour. Statutory regulations lay down that every self-raising flour must yield a minimum quantity of available carbon dioxide during baking.

Plain flour is basically the same but does not contain raising ingredients. It may, therefore, be used in recipes which do not need aeration—sauces, pancakes, short pastries, some cakes (those which depend for their lightness on the air incorporated during preparation), and rich yeast mixtures such as Chelsea buns, tea-breads, etc.

Strong plain flour. 'Strong' refers to the quantity or quality of the protein contained. To mill this flour, a combination of wheats is selected which has a higher protein content than that required for general purpose plain flour. In general terms, the level of protein is controlled according to the purpose for which it is intended the flour will be used. Strong flour is specially milled for breadmaking at home and is also excellent for Yorkshire pudding and rich pastries (puff, rough puff and flaky).

In order to produce loaves with good volume, the proteins in the flour must have a high water-absorption rate and the gluten formed must be capable of being stretched without breaking to give a bold, well-risen loaf with even texture.

Gluten-free Flour

However, there are some people who are allergic to gluten, or for other reasons have to have a gluten-free diet. Some forms of migraine are cured by giving up ordinary flour and substituting gluten-free flour. For these people, special flours have been produced by

Energen Foods Company,
Ashford,
Kent

and

Welfare Foods (Stockport) Ltd.,
63 London Road South,
Poynton,
Stockport,
Cheshire.

Recipes using gluten-free flours can be found on pp. 20 and 52, but for further information and recipes write to the above companies and see the Penguin book of Special Diets, available at most libraries.

Nutregen wheat starch (R.H.M. Energen), Rite-Diet protein-free flour and Rite-Diet gluten-free flour are obtainable at retail chemists and leading health-food stores, and it is worth enquiring whether these products are obtainable on prescription for the dietary management of certain conditions. Most branches of Boots the Chemists keep or will stock these products on request.

Two recipes for gluten-free baking powder can be found on p. 14.

Note: Before following any of the recipes, you will find it very helpful to read the notes on equipment, ingredients and method at the start of the chapters.

Scones

The Basic Scone

The most simple, yet often the most situation-saving form of bread is the scone. It can be baked while the un-expected guest chats—most people are quite happy to watch others at work.

On the other hand, the scone in its own right is the most delicious and economical vehicle for carrying butter, jam, honey or savoury mixtures to the mouth. There seems no end to its versatility.

The scone is so simple to make that very few instructions are necessary: it is merely a large proportion of flour with a little fat and a dash of salt, mixed together with milk or milk-and-water into a 'soft' dough; adding the liquid all at once helps to achieve this effect. You will notice from the recipes that a scone may be made from almost anything you have in the larder, from bits of left-over bacon to the odd home-grown pumpkin or marrow, or the walnuts which drop into your garden from the tree next door. The fat may be anything from best butter to rendered-down trimmings from the Sunday joint or other discarded meat fat, and the ways of sweetening the mixture are numerous; the whole adds up to a most delicious and acceptable offering.

Another advantage of the scone is that a large batch may be baked, placed in a strong plastic bag or polythene container and stored in the deep freeze for long keeping, or the fridge for up to a week, against any unexpected demand which may arise. When you need them, simply pop them into a hot oven for a few minutes.

One of my first jobs was helping to run a Ye Olde Worlde Cake Shoppe in the High Street, Marlborough, and here my first chore of the day was to bake a batch of scones yielding about a gross. These scones were mopped up by gentle old ladies at the rate of knots, and quite frequently more batches would have to be baked during the day. In the beginning, I felt sure that I would never be able to make one batch successfully, but this defeatist attitude soon gave way to a confident, positive approach in which the task became a pleasure. Since that time, and that great lesson in life, I have learnt that not only in cooking is a positive approach to be cultivated!

Ingredients

Flour
Pinch of salt
Fat
Milk and/or water
Raising agents

Additions:

Sugar	Eggs	Orange
Dried fruit	Cheese	Pumpkin
Honey	Bacon	etc.
Syrup	Potatoes	
Treacle		

Equipment

A nice large bowl
A knife, spoons and fork
A rolling pin
A working surface
Sometimes you will need a cutter
A baking tray for cooking them on
An oven or griddle (girdle) or bakestone
A wire rack

About your Ingredients

Flour

Can be plain or self-raising, brown or white, rye or barley, maize or oats: or potatoes can be used in conjunction with flour.

Salt

Brings out the flavour of all the other ingredients. It has been said that a little salt in a sweet dish and a little sugar in a savoury dish improves the flavour throughout.

Fat

The beauty of scone-making is that any fat you happen to have in the house is suitable. All the usual fats can be used — butter, margarine, lard and cooking oil — and a good dripping gives a delicious flavour. To clarify the dripping for this operation, simply melt it with a little water in a saucepan; it can then be strained into a see-through bowl, or simply poured straight in. When set, separate it from the water; if you didn't strain it, simply scrape the bits off the bottom. If the dripping is from chicken, or is any other soft fat, allow it to grow completely cold in the fridge, overnight if necessary, and it will become quite firm enough to handle.

Liquids

These may be water, eggs, milk, milk-and-water, or dried milk powder in conjunction with water, but for the best results there is nothing to equal sour milk or sour cream and water. This gives an added lightness to the texture of the scone—or for that matter to any form of baking in which it is used. Sour milk is not easy to come by since the days of sterilised milk and refrigerators: however, it is very easy to make sour milk for yourself by simply adding a little vinegar and water to fresh milk. Add the vinegar a little at a time until the milk curdles, and then add water or more milk as the recipe requires.

When using sour cream, simply mix it into the dry ingredients with or instead of the fat and use water to moisten the dough. Roughly speaking, scones need $\frac{2}{3}$ pint liquid to 1 lb flour, which seems a lot but is necessary to produce the required soft dough.

Raising Agents—these proportions are for your guidance. To each 8 oz of flour, you may add any one of these combinations:

- Self-raising flour plus 2 level tsps baking powder
- Plain flour plus 4 level tsps baking powder
- Plain flour plus 2 level tsps cream of tartar and 1 level teaspoon bicarbonate of soda
- Plain flour plus 1 level tsp cream of tartar, 1 level tsp bicarbonate of soda, sour milk for mixing

- Plain flour plus 1 level tsp bicarbonate of soda plus 2 tbsps golden syrup (the syrup is used to disguise the colour made by using bicarbonate of soda alone)
- Plain flour plus 1 level tsp bicarbonate of soda plus 1 tbsp vinegar.

You may like to try making your own baking powder. Simply sift all the ingredients together three times and store in an airtight tin.

Baking Powder (1)

A Scottish recipe

4 oz bicarbonate of soda
8 oz cream of tartar
4 oz rice flour

Baking Powder (2)

An Australian recipe

1 lb ground rice
6 oz tartaric acid
8 oz bicarbonate of soda

Gluten-free Baking Powder

3 oz cornflour
$3\frac{1}{2}$ oz bicarbonate of soda
2 oz cream of tartar
2 oz tartaric acid

Special Gluten-free Baking Powder

3 oz Nutregen Wheat Starch
$3\frac{1}{2}$ oz bicarbonate of soda
2 oz cream of tartar
2 oz tartaric acid

Rub the ingredients through a hair sieve.

Special Flour

for scones, teacakes and teabreads etc.

4 lb plain flour
1 oz bicarbonate of soda
2 oz cream of tartar

Additions

Another feature of the scone is that it may be plain, sweet, or savoury, and is thus adaptable to any situation. The additions are numerous, so don't be afraid to try out your own ideas. After all, it is for yourself that you are cooking, so you have only yourself to please.

Proportions

With scones, it hardly matters from the recipe point of view, whether you use more or less sugar, for example; such things are a matter of taste. The important thing, after all, is the basic texture of the dough. The same applies to flour—if you have no scales and instead are using a tablespoon to measure your ingredients, you may find at first that you use too much or too little liquid in proportion, and the dough may suffer a little. Don't let this deter you; the balance can be adjusted by adding a little more flour or a little more water, and though the resulting dough may not be as perfect as you could wish, at least you will have created a product which will surely prove acceptable except to impossibly fussy folk. And if they're not hungry enough to eat what you have made, they're just not hungry!

About your Equipment

The Bowl

Anything which will hold the ingredients and allow room for rubbing-in and/or mixing is adequate. In an emergency a large saucepan can be very useful, but ideally use a nice large bowl so that both hands have freedom to move in the bowl without cramping your style.

Cutlery

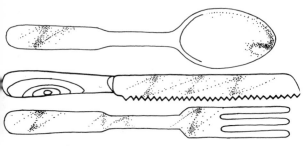

Knife, fork and spoons: most people have their favourite cooking knife and fork, and tablespoon for measuring.

Rolling Pin and Working Surface

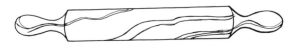

Strictly speaking, a scone is better not rolled but should rather be pressed into shape: however, this is a matter of choice. The working area for rolling out the dough ideally would be one square yard but this is not always possible, and miracles have been worked in much smaller areas. As for a rolling pin, an empty bottle is as good as anything.

Cutter

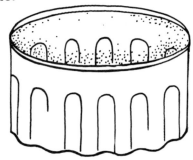

Once the dough is rolled out, it may be shaped into a circle or square and simply cut into eight with a knife. If you prefer, cut it into rounds. If you don't have a proper cutter, you could use a tumbler or handle-less cup, a dried-yeast tin with both ends removed, a jam-jar, an old lid, or anything similar.

Baking Tray

Ideally, a flat baking sheet is the best for the purpose, but thousands of successful scones have been baked in meat tins, sandwich tins, swiss-roll tins, biscuit tin lids, etc. Simply sprinkle the baking tray with flour and arrange the scones quickly and neatly on it.

The Oven

Scone-making is essentially a fairly brisk operation so make sure that the oven is waiting for the scone and not the scone for the oven. Since ovens require different lengths of time for warming-up, you will know from experience at what stage to put the oven on. Generally speaking scones require a 'good' oven, i.e. fairly hot, say

15

400°–450°F, Gas Mark 6–8. When using solid-fuel or oil-fired cookers, the manufacturer's instructions are invariably the safest guide, but since the location of the house (hill or valley, windy or sheltered) sometimes affects the performance of the stove, it is as well to make sure that the oven is really hot before you put your scones in.

For scones cooked on a griddle (girdle) or bakestone, see p. 26.

Cooling Racks

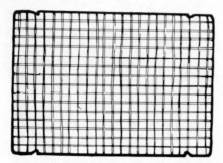

Generally speaking, scones go straight from the baking tray to the table, but should there be an interval, they may be 'aired'. While a proper cooling rack is nice and easy, a clean grill pan with the rack inside may be used, or simply a clean folded tea-towel on a tray. For deep-freezing, the scones must be completely cold.

About the Way you Make your Scones

The method you use for making scones will largely depend on your temperament. If you like things properly done, you will always make time to sift the flour, salt and raising agents together in order to obtain that extra lightness. This is the ideal way and I would suggest that at first you use this method.

However, as you become more experienced and confident, you will, no doubt, if you are busy, become one of the great band of 'bungers-in' who cut out this initial process and get straight into making the dough.

This results in a perfectly satisfactory product for general family consumption, but for purposes of exhibition or competition, remember to use the perfectionists' way.

The experienced 'bunger-in' will achieve as good, or nearly as good, results, simply from the speed with which she completes the operation, as the main object in all scone-making is to finish the job as soon as possible.

The logic of this can be seen clearly if you realise that the proportion of raising agent to the flour is very large, and so the dough must not be kept hanging about or it will start to rise before it is put in the oven, which will result in a heavy texture.

Tips and Tricks-of-the-Trade

- If you are 1 egg short for your recipe, use, instead, 1 level teaspoonful of cornflour—you will never know the difference.
- When no rolling board is available the dough may be rolled out on a sheet of waxed paper. To prevent the paper slipping, moisten the table-top first.
- To make an extra-large width of wax paper, seal two or three pieces together with a hot iron.
  Note: Most breakfast cereals are packeted in waxed paper. It has many uses in the kitchen, and is worth saving.
- A drop of water helps to break up eggs when whisking.

Method for Making Scones

1. *First read your recipe.*
2. Switch on the oven. Collect the ingredients and equipment together in your working area.
3. (optional) Sieve flour, salt and raising agents together into a large bowl.
4. Rub the fat into the flour. This is the most important part of the process—the lightness of the scone is determined by the rubbing-in. To get air into the mixture, lift it high up over the bowl in your fingers, rubbing the fat through the fingertips with the thumbs and allowing the 'crumbs' to drop back into the bowl. This applies particularly if you are making a large batch of scones.
   Note: If you use an electric mixer, be sure to stop the machine **as soon as all the fat has been incorporated** otherwise the resulting texture of the cooked scone will be too dry and crumbly.
5. Add sugar and/or other additions according to the recipe.
6. Add beaten eggs and/or milk and water. Then, using fingertips, mix and knead into a soft ball.
7. Sparingly flour a rolling-out area and, lightly and quickly, press or roll the dough to about $\frac{1}{2}$ in. thickness. If it is higher than this the scone will be too tall and the outside becomes too hard before the middle is cooked.
8. Either:
   —Shape the dough into a round or square and cut into eight
   or
   —Leave the dough whole; dip the selected cutter edge lightly into flour and stamp out firmly, dipping the cutter lightly into the flour again between each stamping. Make sure the cutter goes straight down, otherwise the sides of the scone will topple over. Leave the rounds in place until all the dough-space has been cut out as economically as possible. This operation is very much akin to a dressmaker cutting out her material without wasting it.
9. Pick up the remaining dough and knead it into one piece; press and cut out as before.
10. Slip a knife smartly under each scone and place on the prepared baking tray. It will not matter much if the scones have to touch one another but if the space is adequate, leave a little around each scone.
11. At this point you can glaze the tops if you like. Personally, I never bother because when the scone is eaten it is customary to cut it in half and butter each side and serve butter-side-up on a plate, so the top becomes the bottom and is never seen! However, should you wish for exhibition or competition purposes to glaze the top, simply brush over with milk or milk-and-water or egg yolk and water. But remember that scones cannot wait to go in the oven, so don't take too long over the operation!
12. Place in the preheated oven until cooked. A good test is that the scones should be golden-brown and lift freely off the baking tray.
13. Remove from the oven and cool on a wire rack, or leave on the tray and serve hot or cold, split and buttered.

*The golden rule of scone-making is that the whole operation should be carried out as lightly and speedily as possible.

Note: Scones are a very acceptable contribution to a sale-of-work, fete, or social evening. To make a batch of 70–75 scones you will need the following ingredients:

    3 lb flour (for speed, use self-raising plus 6 level tsps baking powder)
    4–6 oz fat
    1 tsp salt
    Milk and water (nearly 2 pints)
    Sugar, fruit, or other additions as required

Roll or press the dough to $\frac{1}{2}$ in. thick, cut out with a 2 in. cutter (a dried-yeast tin open at both ends is exactly 2 in.) and bake in the usual hot oven. Since sweet scones are usually more acceptable than plain, simply add a little sugar and fruit to the basic scone mixture and adjust the liquid accordingly, to keep a soft consistency.

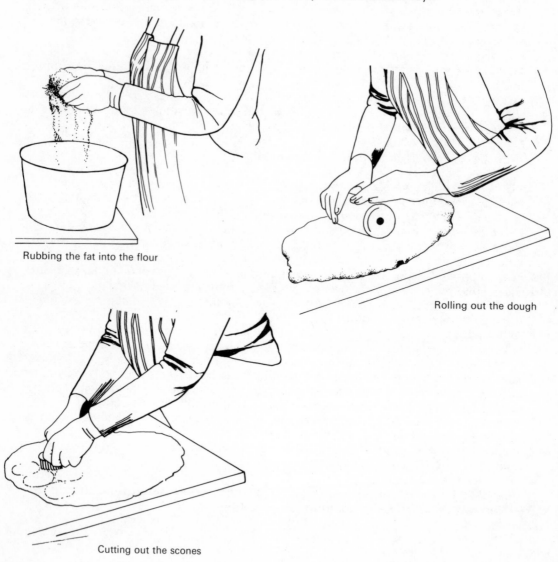

Rubbing the fat into the flour

Rolling out the dough

Cutting out the scones

Plain Oven Scones

Brown Scones

8 oz plain flour
6 oz wholemeal flour
2 oz sugar
3 oz fat
$\frac{1}{2}$ tsp bicarbonate of soda
2 tsps baking powder
Milk to mix

Mix the dry ingredients together. Rub in the fat. Add milk, and mix to a soft dough. Roll out to $\frac{1}{2}$ in. thickness, cut into rounds and bake at 450°F, Mark 8 for about 10 minutes.

Oatcakes

8 oz fine oatmeal
$\frac{1}{2}$ level tsp baking powder
1–2 tbsps hot water
2 oz plain flour
2 oz melted bacon dripping (if you use any other dripping, add a little salt)

Sift together the baking powder and flour and add the oatmeal. Mix well. Add the melted dripping and bind the mixture with 1 tbsp of hot water. Roll out the dough as thinly as possible and, working as quickly as possible, cut into rounds $2\frac{1}{4}$ in. in diameter.

If the dough becomes cool and crumbly before all the oatcakes are made, add the other tablespoon of hot water and make the dough pliable again.

Bake the oatcakes on a lightly greased baking tray at 400°F (Mark 6) for 15 minutes. Lower the heat a little for a further 7–10 minutes.

Store the oatcakes in an airtight tin and serve with butter and cheese. They are also good for breakfast with butter and marmalade or crab apple jelly.

Plain Scones

8 oz plain flour with 4 level tsps baking powder
or
8 oz self-raising flour with 2 level tsps baking powder
$\frac{1}{2}$ tsp salt
$\frac{1}{4}$ pint milk (or milk and water)
$1\frac{1}{2}$ oz butter (or lard, margarine, dripping or a mixture of two or three of these)

Place the flour, salt and baking powder together in a bowl, and rub in the fat. Add the milk all at once and mix, using a round-ended knife, until a soft dough is formed. Turn out onto a **lightly** floured board (too much flour will unbalance the dough recipe) and knead lightly with the fingertips until the dough is smooth. Roll out to $\frac{3}{4}$ in. thickness and cut into rounds, or form into one round and cut into four. Brush with milk or milk and water. Place on a lightly floured baking tray. Bake near the top of the oven at 450°F (Mark 8) for 10 minutes for the small scones, 15 minutes for the large ones.

Scones without Milk

12 oz plain flour
1 tsp bicarbonate of soda
1 tsp cream of tartar
Water to mix
3 tsps sugar
A pinch of salt
A piece of butter the size of a
  walnut
1 egg, well beaten

Sift the dry ingredients together, rub in the butter and mix well with the well-beaten egg, to which a cupful of cold water has been added. Mix to a light dough, cut out and bake at 425°F (Mark 7) for about 15 minutes, or until golden-brown.

Scotch Oven Scones

1 lb plain flour
2 tsps baking powder
1 tsp sugar
½ pint milk
2 oz fine oatmeal
1 tsp salt
1 egg

Sift the flour and baking powder into a basin and add the oatmeal, sugar and salt. Beat the egg until it is pale, and with this and the milk mix the dry ingredients quickly to a smooth dough. Roll out lightly, stamp into rounds with a cutter, brush over the tops with a little milk, and bake at 425°F (Mark 7) for 15 minutes.

Gluten-free Scones

for special gluten-free diets

This recipe may be used for oven or griddle scones

16 oz Rite-Diet gluten-free flour
1 heaped tbsp gluten-free baking
  powder
4 fluid oz milk
4 oz sugar
2 eggs, beaten
4 oz butter or margarine
4–5 oz currants, sultanas or chopped
  cherries

Sift the Rite-Diet flour and gluten-free baking powder together, and rub in the fat. Dissolve the sugar in a mixture made from the milk and the beaten eggs and add the fruit. Add to the fat and flour and mix to a soft dough. Drop the mixture with a dessertspoon onto a greased baking sheet, brush lightly with egg or milk and bake at 425°F (Mark 7) until golden and firm,

or

allow the dough to stand for 30 minutes, knead gently on a well-dusted board and roll out to ½ in. thickness. Cut into shapes, place on greased tins and finish as above.

Note: *This scone mixture may be used for Scotch pancakes. Simply omit the fruit and bake on a hot-plate.*

Sweet Oven Scones

Devonshire Treacle Scones

From Mr. A. N., living near Exeter

8 oz self-raising flour
1 oz sugar (optional)
$\frac{1}{2}$ tsp bicarbonate of soda
1 tsp mixed spice
$1\frac{1}{2}$ oz butter
2 oz black treacle
$\frac{1}{2}$ tsp cream of tartar

Warm the treacle; mix all the other ingredients together. Pour the warmed treacle onto the mixture and knead well. Cut into the shapes required, and place on a floured baking tray. Glaze with milk or egg and bake for 20 minutes at 350°F (Mark 4). Serve while still hot.

Dublin Wholemeal Date Teascones

From Miss Walker, Eire

1 lb wheaten-meal flour
1 level tsp bicarbonate of soda
1 level tsp cream of tartar
1 level tsp salt
8 oz stoned dates, chopped as small as sultanas
6 tsps castor sugar
3 oz butter (or margarine)
Buttermilk (or milk and water, or all milk) to mix

Mix well together the wheaten-meal, bicarbonate of soda, cream of tartar and salt. Rub in the fat, mix in the sugar, add the chopped dates and mix. Add sufficient buttermilk to knead to a firm dough (slightly softer than for bread). Cut in triangles and bake at 375°F (Mark 5) for about 20 minutes.

These scones are delicious served hot, with butter, for tea.

Isle of Man Scones

8 oz self-raising flour
$1\frac{1}{2}$ heaped tsps baking powder
A pinch of salt
3 oz sugar
2 oz sultanas
Milk and water to mix
$2\frac{1}{2}$ oz margarine
$\frac{1}{4}$ tsp bicarbonate of soda (dissolved in a drop of hot water)

Mix the dry ingredients together and rub in the margarine. Mix to a soft dough with the liquids. Bake at 425°F (Mark 7) for 15–20 minutes.

Pumpkin Scones

From Weipa Mission Station, Queensland, from a book sold in aid of a fund to prevent the Queensland Aborigines from dying out

12 oz plain flour
1 teacupful boiled and mashed pumpkin or marrow
$\frac{1}{4}$ pint milk
1 tsp cream of tartar
1 tsp bicarbonate of soda
$1\frac{1}{2}$ oz butter
$1\frac{1}{2}$ oz sugar
A pinch of salt

Beat the butter, sugar and pumpkin together and add the milk with the bicarbonate of soda dissolved in it. Sift the flour with the cream of tartar and add to the rest of the ingredients. Roll out and cook at 375°F (Mark 5) until golden brown and cooked through.

Strawberry Scones

For the scones

1 lb plain flour
4 tsps sugar
3 tsps baking powder
½ tsp salt
3 oz margarine
Milk to mix

For the strawberry mixture

Strawberries as required (approx. 12 oz)
2 tbsps sugar
2 tbsps water

Sift the flour, baking powder, salt and sugar together. Quickly rub in the fat and add just sufficient milk to make a soft dough. Roll out lightly, dust the top sparingly with flour and fold one half over the other. Cut into two rounds, and place in greased sandwich tins. Bake at 425°F (Mark 7) for 15–20 minutes. Leave to cool a little in the tins, but loosen the top part of each round (they should come apart where they were folded over after rolling).

Make a little syrup for the strawberries with the sugar and water. Bring to the boil, boil for 2 minutes and then lay in the strawberries and cook for 4 minutes, making sure that the strawberries are hot right through. Remove the top part of each scone round, spread the hot strawberries on the base, replace the tops and sprinkle with sugar. Cut into sections and serve at once.

Sussex Lardy Johns

8 oz plain flour
A pinch of salt
1 tsp baking powder
4 oz lard
2 oz sugar
4 oz currants
Water for mixing

Mix the salt and baking powder with the flour. Rub in the lard, then add the sugar and currants and sufficient water to make a stiff dough. Roll this dough out on a floured board until it is fairly thin, then cut into squares. Place the squares on a floured baking tray and bake at 425°F (Mark 7) for approximately 10 minutes.

Canadian Tea Cakes

From a Victorian booklet entitled 'Five-O'clock Tea', published in 1887. For interest, all details are included as in the original publication.

				s.	d.
1 lb flour	..	..	..	0	2½
½ pint of milk	..	..	..	0	1
2 oz of butter	..	..	..	0	2
¼ lb of sugar	..	..	..	0	1
2 oz of currants		..	..	0	0½
2 eggs	..	..	..	0	2
1 teaspoonful of baking powder		..	..	0	0½
				0	9½

Time, half an hour.

1. Take a clean basin.
2. Put one pound of flour into it.
3. Rub into the flour one heaped teaspoonful of baking powder.
4. Then rub in two ounces of butter.
5. Wash, dry and pick 2 ozs of currants.
6. Add a quarter of a pound of pounded sugar (granulated sugar came later).
7. Add the currants to the other ingredients.
8. Well beat the two eggs with:
9. Half a pint of milk.
10. Mix everything together.
11. Flour a paste board.
12. Roll out the dough.
13. Form into teacakes.
14. Bake on a buttered tin in a moderate oven.
15. When half done, wash over with the yolk of an egg beaten in a teaspoon of milk.
16. Bake till done, then cut in slices and butter.
17. Serve hot.

Walnut and Cinnamon Scones

1 lb plain flour
2 tsps baking powder
A pinch of salt
2 oz butter
1 egg, beaten
Milk to mix
1 tbsp sugar
1 tsp ground cinnamon
2 tbsps chopped walnuts

Mix the flour, baking powder and salt; rub in the fat. Add the egg and sufficient milk to make a soft dough. Now take the sugar, cinnamon and walnuts, and sprinkle over the dough. Fold the dough in three. Roll out lightly to ¾ in. thickness. Cut into shapes as required and bake at 400°F (Regulo 6) until golden-brown.

Wigs

1 lb plain flour
2 tsps baking powder
A pinch of salt
6 oz butter, lard or margarine
1 oz sugar
2 oz currants
2 oz chopped mixed peel
1 egg, beaten
Approximately ¼ pint milk to mix

Mix the baking powder and salt with the flour, rub in the fat and add all the other ingredients, using enough milk to form a stiff dough. Roll out fairly thinly on a floured board and cut into large rounds (traditionally wigs were saucer-sized). Place these on a well-greased baking tray and bake at 425°F (Mark 7) for about 20 minutes, or until well cooked.

Wigs should be eaten hot, split and covered with butter.

Savoury Oven Scones

Countess Hilda's Cheese Scones

5 oz self-raising flour
5 oz grated cheese
A pinch of salt
1 oz butter or margarine
A little milk to mix
¼ tsp dry mustard

Mix together the flour, cheese, mustard and salt. Rub in the fat. Mix to a soft dough with the milk. Cut into 2 in. rounds and bake for 8 minutes in the centre of the oven at 450°F (Mark 8).

Durham Cheese Scones

1 lb self-raising flour
4 oz margarine
4 oz cheese (Cheddar)
A good pinch of salt
A pinch of dry mustard (optional)
½ pint milk and water to mix

Rub the margarine into the flour and stir in the grated cheese. Mix to a soft dough with the milk and water. Roll out on a floured board to ½ in. thick and cut into rounds, using a 2 in. cutter. Bake for 10 minutes at 475°F (Mark 9), third runner from the top.

Potato Oven Scones

6 oz mashed potato
8 oz plain flour
A pinch of salt
3 oz butter or margarine
Water to mix

Mix the salt into the flour and rub in the butter. Add the potato and mix well. Pour in just enough water to make a stiff dough. Roll the dough out on a well-floured board, to about 1 in. thickness, and cut into small rounds with a pastry cutter. Bake at 450°F (Mark 8) for about 10 minutes, or until nicely brown.

These scones should be split and served with butter.

Sardine Scones

Scones

4 oz plain flour + 2 level tsps baking
   powder
or
4 oz self-raising flour + ½ level tsp
   baking powder
½ level tsp salt
¾ oz fat (lard, margarine or dripping)
About 3 tbsp milk

Filling

Small tin sardines
Cayenne pepper
Salt to taste
A few drops of lemon juice or
   vinegar

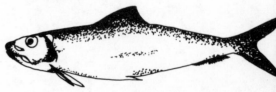

Mix flour, baking powder and salt; rub in the fat. Add the milk and mix to a soft dough. Turn onto a lightly-floured board, and pat and roll it into about ½ in. thickness; then cut into rounds. Place these on a lightly-greased tin and bake for 10–15 minutes at 425°F (Mark 7).

While the scones are baking, mix the contents of a tin of sardines with cayenne papper, salt (if liked) and lemon juice or vinegar, and mash to a spreading consistency.

Remove the scones from the oven and while they are still hot split them and spread the sardine mixture on the bases. Replace the tops, decorate when cool with watercress or mustard and cress, and serve with a green salad.

Scottish Breakfast Cheese Rolls

1 lb plain flour
2 oz wheatmeal flour
2 tsps cream of tartar
1 tsp baking soda
1 tsp salt
4 oz sugar
3 oz butter or margarine
2 eggs
Milk
Some finely grated cheese

Mix the flours, salt, raising agents and sugar and rub in the fat with your fingertips. Beat the eggs and add sufficient egg and milk to make a soft dough, retaining a little egg and milk for brushing over the rolls.

Roll the dough out lightly on a floured board and cut into rounds ¼ in. thick. Brush the edges of these rounds with the egg and milk. Sprinkle on the cheese, fold over double and brush with egg and milk.

Bake on a greased baking sheet at 425°F (Mark 7) for 15 minutes.

Cheese Muffins

6 oz plain flour
1½ oz cheese, grated
¼ tsp salt
4 tsps baking powder
1 egg
4 fluid oz milk

Beat the egg lightly and add the salt and milk. Mix the flour and baking powder together, then add the grated cheese. Make into a dough with the liquid, beat well and roll out. Cut into rounds, brush with beaten egg, and bake for 10 minutes at 425°F (Mark 7). These muffins are delicious split, spread with butter and eaten hot.

Bacon Muffins

A Dutch recipe

8 oz plain flour
1 oz sugar
3 tbsps melted fat
¼ pint milk
3 tsps baking powder
½ tsp salt
1 egg
½ cup crispy bits of bacon

Sift together the flour, sugar, salt and baking powder. Add the beaten egg and milk. Add the melted fat and beat in quickly. Stir in the bits of crispy bacon. Pour into deep patty tins or Yorkshire pudding tins, and bake at 425°F (Mark 7) for 15–20 minutes. Traditionally, serve with orange marmalade.

These muffins can also be cooked on a griddle (see p. 26).

Making Scones on a Griddle

Griddle, Girdle, Bakestone or Welsh Plank

The Concise Oxford Dictionary describes the bakestone as 'a flat stone, slate, or iron plate, on which cakes are baked'. A griddle or girdle is 'a circular iron plate hung over fire for toasting cakes'; a Welsh plank is the same.

Although these objects are associated with the very early forms of cooking, long before ovens were used, they are now being manufactured for the modern house-wife. One bought recently had a long saucepan-like handle instead of the tra-ditional semi-circular handle for hanging, which makes handling much easier and less daunting. Scones cooked in this fashion are quick to cook, delicious to eat and very convenient, especially if you have no oven or, wishing to be economical, prefer to avoid heating a whole oven only for scones. Cooking in this fashion also has instant appeal to the dramatic in any audience you may have acquired. But be prepared for demand to exceed supply on occasion!

The idea of making scones on a griddle may be a completely novel one to you, and one which you may very well like to try. Before going out and buying a griddle, I suggest that you try your hand at making a batch in a thick frying pan, on the solid plate of an electric cooker, or on the cooler plate of a solid-fuel cooker. If you have a gas cooker, cover the flame with an asbestos sheet, and rest your heavy frying pan on that.

Two types of modern griddle

There are two types of griddle scone, as you will notice from the recipes. One is an ordinary scone mixture pressed or rolled out, cut into convenient shapes and simply cooked on a greased griddle instead of in the oven. The other type of scone which may be cooked on a griddle is made from a batter—this is called a pancake or drop-scone, since the mixture is dropped in spoonsful onto the lightly greased griddle. The texture of the mixture should be that of thick cream, and in this respect oil or melted fat, which are often included in the ingredients, seem to make a more velvety consistency and a much improved scone.

The heat of the griddle differs for the two different types of scone; drop-scones are best cooked on a hot greased griddle, but rolled-out scones need a lower temperature. Rolled-out griddle scones require about 7 minutes each side in order to cook through. Drop-scones take less time, and should be turned as the bubbles

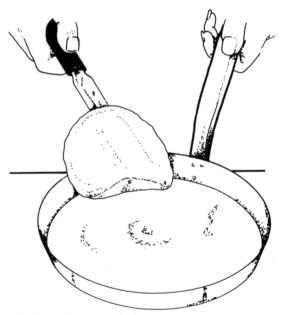

Turning a drop-scone in the pan

begin to form. They may be kept hot in a clean folded tea towel as this helps to retain the moisture.

The ingredients and equipment are the same for griddle scones and pancakes as for oven scones, but it is necessary in addition to have a palette knife or suitable fish-slice for turning the scones over on the griddle.

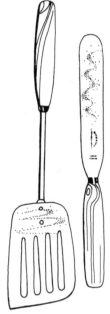

Many successful parties have been held using griddle scones as the basic dish. Children, in particular, enjoy such parties and may be co-opted into helping if tall enough to reach the griddle and sufficiently responsible in attitude.

Warning! One word of warning: more accidents occur in the home than in the whole of industry. May I, therefore, urge you to take particular care when greasing the hot-plate of an electric stove. Please use the fat very sparingly, and be prepared to switch off immediately should the need arise.

To Test the Heat of the Griddle

Heat the griddle and sprinkle a little dry flour upon it. In a few minutes it should become golden-brown: if the flour becomes dark very quickly, the griddle is too hot.

Good griddling!

Plain Griddle Scones

Simple Irish Potato Cakes

8 oz mashed potato
A pinch of salt
1 oz flour

Mix all the ingredients together well until a stiff dough is formed. Roll this out on a well-floured board and cut into squares. Grease a girdle or thick frying pan and cook the potato cakes until they are golden-brown on both sides.

These cakes should be split while they are hot and spread with butter.

Oatcakes

$\frac{1}{4}$ tsp bicarbonate of soda
A pinch of salt
2 breakfastcups fine oatmeal
1 oz lard
$\frac{1}{4}$ pint hot water

Mix the bicarbonate of soda and salt with the oatmeal. Rub in the lard, and use sufficient hot water to mix to a stiff dough. Roll this out until very thin on a board which has been well dusted with oatmeal.

Cut into teaplate-sized rounds, then cut into quarters to make fan-shaped pieces. Heat and grease a griddle and cook the oatcakes until they are brown on both sides.

These oatcakes are eaten cold with lashings of butter.

Simple Scotch Griddle Scones

1 lb plain flour
1 small tsp salt
1 small tsp bicarbonate of soda
1 tsp cream of tartar
Milk to mix (sour milk or buttermilk
   is best—see p. 13)
Note: If sweet milk is used, 1$\frac{1}{2}$ tsps
   cream of tartar will be required

Sift the ingredients; mix in a bowl with the milk till the dough comes clean from the bowl. Knead and roll out to a thickness of $\frac{1}{2}$ in. and cut in squares. Lay on a warm floured griddle (or iron frying pan). When brown, turn.

Teisen Ar Y Maen

(Literally 'Cake-on-the-Stone' or Bake-stone Cake)

A very old Welsh recipe

3 tbsps dripping (bacon is good)
6 oz plain flour
3 tbsps sugar

28

1 small tsp bicarbonate of soda
3 fluid oz sour milk or buttermilk (or fresh milk with ½ tsp vinegar added)
1 egg, beaten

Rub the fat into the flour and sugar. Mix the bicarbonate of soda with the milk and beaten egg. Mix all together to a dryish dough. Roll out on a lightly-floured board until wafer thin, and cut into rounds. Bake on a hot greased griddle, turning when brown—a thick-bottomed frying pan will do.

Butter, and eat while hot.

Welsh Light Cakes

A traditional Welsh recipe used by Mrs. Marion Roberts, when living on a remote hill farm in the mountains of Merioneth-shire, North Wales

1 small egg
½ tsp bicarbonate of soda
4 fluid oz buttermilk or sour cream
8 oz self-raising flour
A pinch of salt

Whisk the egg, mix the bicarbonate of soda with the buttermilk or cream, and mix all the ingredients together to the consistency of Yorkshire pudding batter. Heat a frying pan, rub it with lard and drop in table-spoons of the mixture. Fry until brown on one side, turn and brown the other side. Put on a dish, add a generous dab of butter to each cake, and place in the oven to keep warm. Make another batch of cakes and put them on top of the first, and so on, layer upon layer until all the mixture is used up.

Serve very hot with sugar or syrup over them.

Sweet Griddle Scones

Kentish Oast House Cakes

1 lb plain flour
4 oz lard
A pinch of salt
8 oz currants
1 tsp baking powder
2 oz sugar
Water to mix
1 tsp lemon juice

Mix the baking powder and flour, add the sugar and salt and rub in the lard until the mixture resembles fine breadcrumbs. Add the lemon juice and sufficient water to make a light dough and finally add the currants. Roll the dough out on a well-floured board and cut into rounds. Cook on a griddle until the cakes are golden in colour on both sides, and then serve while hot.

Scotch Girdle Scones

8 oz plain flour
½ tsp bicarbonate of soda
½ tsp cream of tartar
1 oz lard or butter
1 tsp golden syrup
¼ pint sour milk (or fresh milk plus ½ tsp extra of cream of tartar)

Rub the fat into the dry ingredients after sieving them together. Add the milk to the syrup, pour onto the mixture and mix to a soft dough. Divide the dough into 2 rounds about ½ in. thick and cut each round into 4. Cook on the ready-heated girdle until light brown, turning at intervals until sufficiently brown and cooked.

Singin' Hinnies

These griddle cakes come from Northumberland. Their name is derived from the fact that they make a soft singing noise as they cook. It is essential that you eat them while they are hot.

1 lb plain flour
$\frac{1}{2}$ tsp cream of tartar
$\frac{1}{4}$ tsp bicarbonate of soda
A pinch of salt
4 oz butter
4 oz lard
Milk to mix
8 oz currants

Mix the cream of tartar, bicarbonate of soda and salt into the flour. Rub in the butter and lard and pour in sufficient milk to make a stiff dough. Finally, mix in the currants. Roll into a ball and then flatten out to $\frac{1}{2}$ in. thickness. Rub a little fat over the top of the griddle and cook the cake until it is brown on both sides.

Eat while hot—cut into pieces, split and spread with butter.

Bearpark Girdle Scones

1 lb plain flour
1 tsp salt
1 egg (optional)
2 oz sugar
$\frac{3}{4}$ tsp bicarbonate of soda
$1\frac{1}{2}$ tsps cream of tartar
2 oz margarine
Milk to mix (if sour milk is used, use only half the quantity of cream of tartar)

Rub the fat into the dry ingredients, and make a soft dough with the egg and/or milk. Knead lightly on a floured board to make a smooth ball. Roll out to $\frac{1}{4}$ in. thick. Cut across in 8 pieces or cut into rounds. Place on a hot girdle to bake until well risen and a light brown underneath. Turn the scones onto the other side and cook until the centre is dry.

Cacen Gri

5 oz margarine, lard or dripping
9 oz plain flour
A pinch of salt
6 tbsps sugar
1 cup sultanas
1 cup currants
1 small cup milk
1 tbsp vinegar
1 egg, beaten
$\frac{1}{2}$ tsp cream of tartar
$\frac{1}{2}$ tsp bicarbonate of soda

Rub the fat into the flour and add the salt, sugar and fruit. Mix the milk and vinegar with the egg, add the cream of tartar and bicarbonate of soda and mix into the flour mixture.

Knead with your fingers, then turn onto a board and roll out to $\frac{1}{4}$ in. thick, or less if possible. Cut into rounds, and cook both sides on a moderately hot girdle, griddle or thick frying pan.

Eat hot, spread with butter.

Honey Cream Scones

5 fluid oz sour milk (or buttermilk or
  milk with a tsp of vinegar)
6 tbsp honey, or sugar, or half and
  half
1 egg, unbeaten
14 oz plain flour (unbleached white
  or half white, half wholewheat)
1 heaped tsp baking soda
2 heaped tsps cream of tartar
$\frac{1}{2}$ cup melted butter

Mix together the milk, sugar and egg. Sift in
the flour with the raising agents. Beat well
and then gradually add the melted butter.
Keep the dough moist, but if necessary add
up to 2 oz more flour for rolling out. Roll
out to just under $\frac{1}{2}$ in. thick, cut into
triangles and dust with flour. Bake slowly
on a greased griddle or thick frying pan for
5–7 minutes, making sure that the middle
is cooked.

*Serve hot with butter and honey, or
cold with Cornish cream and honey, or
just with butter—these scones are plenty
sweet enough.*

Note: *Raisins, nuts or dates may be
added to this recipe.*

Welsh Cakes

8 oz self-raising flour
4 oz butter
2 tbsps sugar
4 oz currants
1 small egg
A pinch of salt
$2\frac{1}{2}$ fluid oz buttermilk or sour milk

Rub the fat into the flour, add the sugar
and currants. Beat the egg and salt, add
the buttermilk, and mix together to a stiff
paste. Put the frying pan onto the heat and
rub with lard. While it is heating, roll out
the cake mixture on a floured board to
$\frac{1}{2}$ in. thick, cut into rounds with a pastry
cutter or top of a glass, put into the pan
and cook until brown on one side; then
turn and brown the other side.

*While they are nicer eaten hot, they can
be split and buttered when cold, or toasted
and buttered.*

Cumberland Girdle Scones

From Mrs. E. Birkett

1 lb plain flour
2 good tsps baking powder
$\frac{1}{2}$ tsp salt
1 tbsp sugar
2 oz lard
2 eggs, beaten
Water to make eggs up to $\frac{1}{2}$ pint

Mix the flour, baking powder and salt. Rub
in the lard and add the sugar. Mix to a
stiff paste with the egg-and-water. Chop
the paste vigorously with a knife, and then
reshape into a cake, handling the dough as
little as possible. Cut into 6 pieces, roll
each piece into a round and cut into 4.
Bake on a fairly hot, well-greased griddle.

Serve with jam.

Batter Griddle Scones, Pancakes and Drop-Scones

Pikelets

1½ oz sugar
A pinch of salt
8 oz plain flour
½ tsp bicarbonate of soda
Buttermilk or sour milk to mix (see
   p. 13)
Oil for frying

Mix the sugar and salt with the flour, and make a well in the centre. Dissolve the bicarbonate of soda in a little of the milk, and pour this into the flour mixture. Add sufficient milk to mix to a good batter; beat well. Heat some oil in a frying pan, then cook small quantities of the batter as you would pancakes. They can also be cooked on a griddle or girdle.

Pikelets should be served hot, spread with lots of butter.

Corn Griddle Cakes

4 oz plain flour
2 oz wheatmeal flour
Approx. 6 fluid oz milk
¾ cupful tinned sweetcorn, drained
3 tsps baking powder
3 tbsps sugar
1 egg

Sift together the flour, meal, baking powder, sugar and salt. Beat the egg, add to the milk and stir in the corn. Mix lightly with the dry ingredients and beat well. Bake in large tablespoonsful on a greased griddle (or girdle), keeping the batter shapes as round as possible. When bubbles show on top and the cakes are lightly brown underneath, turn them and cook lightly on the other side.

Serve buttered, hot.

Note: *For a tasty savoury version of this 'cake' leave out sugar, season with pepper and salt, and serve hot with bacon or sausages.*

Durham Drop Scones

6 tbsps self-raising flour
2 tbsps sugar
½ tsp salt
A knifeful of syrup
1 egg, beaten
Milk to mix

Mix the dry ingredients together and add the syrup and beaten egg. Mix to a fairly thick batter with a little milk. Cook on a hotplate or in a thick frying pan, turning when bubbles appear on the surface.

Grandma Jones' Wild Raspberry Griddle Scones

Maisie Jones told me this story about her old Grandma who lived in West Wales on a small farm. One hot summer's day she and her Grandma, her mother and the other children had all been out working in the fields and were walking home, weary, and the children were saying that they were 'starving', when they came across some wild raspberries. Quick as a flash, Grandma Jones picked as many as she could, telling the children that they should have a rare treat if they would gather all the fruit. So they all set to and carried them home in a hanky. No sooner home than the old lady, 'quick as a little robin', put the griddle to heat on the fire while she collected an egg, some flour, etc., and Maisie said that within a few minutes they were all seated and eating these mouth-watering scones, burning their mouths because they were so good. She couldn't give the exact recipe so here is my version which I made with, of course, garden raspberries. Strawberries are a delicious alternative.

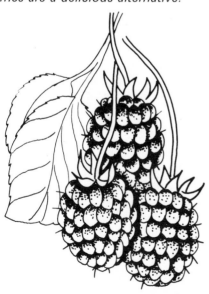

1 egg
4 oz self-raising flour
A pinch of salt
Sour milk to mix (see p. 13)
$\frac{1}{2}$ tsp baking powder
or
$\frac{1}{2}$ tsp bicarbonate of soda
A handful of raspberries or
    strawberries—say 4–6 oz or more

Beat the first five ingredients together to form a batter, which should be thicker than cream but looser than mayonnaise. Have your griddle pan hot and greased with an all-over smear of fat ready for cooking. Now, there are two ways of cooking: the fruit can be mixed into the batter *or* the batter can be put into the pan and the fruit dropped onto the scone before the top is too set. Either way is good, but don't make the scones too big or you won't keep up with the demand! Sprinkle the scone with sugar after having turned it in the pan to cook the second side a little—not too much on account of the fruit which needn't be really cooked—and slide onto a hot plate.

Pikelets Welsh

$2\frac{1}{2}$ oz self-raising flour
1 tbsp beaten egg
$\frac{1}{4}$ pint milk
2 oz sugar
2 tsps baking powder
1 tsp Birds egg powder (if liked)

Mix all the ingredients together to form a batter. Cook on a Welsh plank (griddle or girdle), on the cool plate of an Aga cooker, or in a thick-bottomed frying pan as you would pancakes. Use grease for the first batch only.

Can be served buttered or spread with jam for tea.

33

Rice Griddle Cakes

4 oz plain flour
½ tsp baking powder
1 tsp salt
1 teacup boiled rice (or leftover rice
    pudding—remove skin)
1 egg
1 tbsp melted butter
¼ pint top of the milk
Nutmeg to taste

Mix flour, baking powder, salt, rice and
nutmeg (if liked) together. Mix together
the egg, butter and milk, and add to the
dry ingredients until you have a smooth
batter. Cook in spoonsful on a hot,
greased griddle, turning once.

Scotch Pancakes

6 oz plain flour
2 tsps cream of tartar
1 egg
4 oz sugar
¼ pint milk
1 tsp bicarbonate of soda

Mix the flour and cream of tartar together.
Beat the egg with the sugar. Dissolve the
bicarbonate of soda in the milk, and add to
the egg and sugar mixture. Add this liquid
to the dry ingredients and beat. Drop in
small quantities onto a hot, greased
griddle and cook as for pancakes.

Orange Wholewheat Hotcakes

2½ tbsps oil
½ tsp baking soda
8 oz wholewheat flour
2 eggs
½ tsp salt
2 cups freshly squeezed orange juice

Mix the eggs and oil, and beat together.
Add the dry ingredients and orange juice
alternately to the egg and oil mixture until
well blended. Cook in spoonsful on a
griddle or in a thick-bottomed frying pan.

*Eat hot with butter and/or marmalade
for breakfast. A little sugar may be added
to the recipe if desired.*

Scots Crumpets

4 eggs, separated
½ pint milk
2 oz sugar
6 oz plain flour

Mix the egg yolks, milk, sugar and flour.
Beat the egg whites stiffly and fold into
the mixture. Bake on a bakestone or griddle,
turning once. Sprinkle with sugar to
serve.

Unyeasted Breads

'A loaf of bread', the Walrus said,
'Is what we chiefly need . . .'

'Through the Looking Glass' by Lewis Carroll

Although it is no longer true to say that in the British nation 'everything stops for tea' in the old traditional way, there are still those occasions when there is a call for something to fill a gap, to entertain a visitor, or to contribute to a social function.

The exciting thing about making these easy breads is that almost any ingredient one has in the larder may be used, as the basis for them is simply flour, liquid, fat and, in some recipes, sugar.

In fact, these loaves may be plain—without sugar, eggs or fat—they may be semi-sweet, or they can be unashamedly rich for special treats. For this reason, you will find that the recipes have been classified for your guidance.

This bread has the added advantage of storing well in the deep freeze without taking up too much space, and we all know how useful it is to have such a stand-by in case of unexpected visitors.

About your Equipment and Ingredients

With few exceptions, the equipment and ingredients necessary for making these recipes are the same as for scones.

The main difference is that a loaf tin is used instead of a baking sheet, but cake tins or oven-proof dishes may be used, or even old saucepans without handles, the only important thing being that they are well-greased.

About your Method

There are several ways to make these breads.

1. The plain method—put everything in together and mix
2. The soaking method—soak the fruit in cold tea, or whatever is recommended, overnight
3. The rubbing-in method
4. The method which involves melting fat in water
5. The beating creaming method, for richer mixtures.

Given a chance, these recipes will encourage you to be adventurous; for instance, Banana Bread is unexpectedly delicious even for those who do not very much care for bananas! It is a very good way of using up over-ripe bananas, and deep-freezes extremely well, so you need never again extravagantly throw out bananas which have overstayed their welcome.

***Tip**: When soaking fruit for Brack or Bara Brith type tea-breads, a convenient and economical way, which helps you finish up that last inaccessible bit of jam or marmalade at the bottom of the jar, is to put alternate layers of tea and dried fruit in the jar and leave it to soak. The jam or marmalade seems to improve the flavour and nothing is wasted. The tea, of course, is simply what has been left over in the teapot.

Plain Unyeasted Breads

Instant Breakfast Bread

The most useful recipe I know. For use in emergencies, on that day when some starving soul has raided the breadbin after coming home late at night, leaving not one crumb for the rest of the family. This bread is also most acceptable when unexpected guests arrive for tea.

Take (roughly) a handful of self-raising flour per person, salt in proportion (about 1 level tsp per 1 lb of flour), mix with a fork and add milk, or milk and water, or better still, sour milk (p. 13), until a soft dough is obtained. Knead lightly for a minute or so, then cut into 3 or 4, roll around neatly and swiftly and place on a hot, floured baking tray. If time allows before baking, cut a cross on the top with a sharp knife and dab over with a little milk or water. Bake at 375–400°F (Mark 5–6) until lightly browned. Cool slightly before cutting or breaking open.

Note: *The mixture can be used for breakfast rolls by dividing into more portions. About 20 rolls may be made with 1 lb of flour.*

Quick Soda Bread

From a Kentish farmer's wife

1 lb wholemeal flour
About $\frac{3}{4}$ pint milk, sour if possible (see p. 13)
1 level tsp salt
1 level tsp bicarbonate of soda
1 level tsp cream of tartar

Warm the flour and put it in a warm bowl with the other dry ingredients. Allow it to trickle through your fingers to aerate. Mix with the milk, using a knife, until the dough rolls out of the bowl cleanly. Turn onto a well-floured board, cut in half and quickly shape each piece, rolling in flour. Don't handle too much or the bread will be 'mean and close'. Bake on a greased baking sheet for 45 minutes at 375°F (Mark 5), reducing after 20 minutes to 300°F (Mark 1 or 2).

Rolled Oats and Rye Bread

1 lb wholewheat flour
8 oz rye flour
2 cups rolled or porridge oats
$\frac{1}{2}$–$\frac{3}{4}$ pint water, to mix
1 tbsp corn oil or dripping, lard, margarine or butter
1 tbsp sesame oil
2 tsps salt

Mix the flours, rub in the oil or fat and mix in the salt. Add the water gradually, until all the flour is moistened and the dough is kneadable. Knead well, 300 times, then shape into 1 large or 2 smaller loaves, making cuts across the tops. Leave overnight to prove, or for 2–6 hours, depending on the temperature of the room. Bake at 425°F (Mark 7) for 30 minutes, then lower the heat to 375°F (Mark 5) and continue baking for 45 minutes to 1 hour.

Sweet Unyeasted Breads

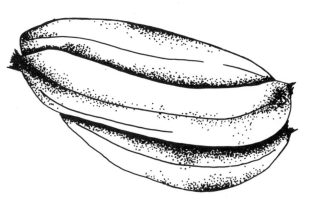

Cake Bread

The basic cake loaf from which all others stem

8 oz self-raising flour
2 oz sugar, brown for preference
4 oz treacle
$\frac{1}{4}$ pint milk
$1\frac{1}{2}$ oz lard
$\frac{1}{2}$ tsp salt
1 level tsp bicarbonate of soda
1 level tsp mixed spice
$\frac{1}{2}$ tsp cinnamon

Sieve the dry ingredients together. Warm the syrup, milk, lard and sugar until the lard is melted. Stir the liquid into the dry ingredients until all are blended; don't beat. Place in a greased and floured 6 in. tin and bake in the centre of the oven at 350°F (Mark 4) for $1\frac{1}{4}$ hours, or until a knitting needle or orange stick comes out dry and clean. Leave for a few minutes in the tin, then cool on a rack.

Serve sliced thinly and buttered.

Banana Loaf

7 oz plain flour
4 oz sugar
1 oz margarine
1 oz lard
A pinch of salt
3 oz chopped walnuts
1 level tsp baking powder
$\frac{1}{2}$ tsp bicarbonate of soda
3 bananas—if small, add 1 tbsp milk

Brush a 1 lb loaf tin with melted fat and line the base with greaseproof paper. Sift the flour, bicarbonate of soda, baking powder and salt into a dish. Rub the fats into the flour mixture and add the sugar and chopped walnuts. Mash the bananas and add to the mixture to form a dropping consistency. Turn the mixture into the prepared tin and bake at 350°F (Mark 4) for 30 minutes. Reduce the heat to 310°F (Mark 2) and bake for a further 45 minutes or until the loaf is well risen and firm in the centre.

Maltless Malt Loaf

From Edna Eastham, Caerfarchell, Nr. St. Davids, Pembs.

8 oz brown flour
4 oz white self-raising flour
Chopped nuts (optional)
1 tsp bicarbonate of soda
7 fluid oz milk
8 oz sugar
1 cup sultanas
1 tsp salt
1 tbsp syrup
2 oz butter

Warm the butter, milk and syrup in a pan. Sieve into a mixing bowl the dry ingredients, except for the bicarbonate of soda, which must be added to the milk mixture. Add the milk mixture to the dry ingredients and mix well. Put into 2 greased 1 lb loaf tins and bake at 300°F (Mark 1–2) for 1½ hours, and then 250°F (Mark ¼) for a further 30 minutes.

Not to be cut until the following day. Serve in slices, preferably buttered.

Prune and Nut Loaf

8 oz self-raising flour
¼ tsp salt
3 oz soft brown sugar
½ tsp ground ginger
2 oz butter or margarine
4 oz stoned prunes, chopped
2 oz chopped walnuts
Milk to mix

Grease and flour a loaf tin. Mix the flour, salt and sugar and rub in the fat. Add the ginger, nuts and prunes and sufficient milk to make a soft, dropping dough. Turn into the tin and bake for 45–50 minutes at 350°F (Mark 4).

Quick Bread

1 large breakfast-cup plain flour
1 large breakfast cup wholemeal
   flour
1 tbsp baking powder
1 tsp salt
1 good tsp syrup
1 breakfast-cup milk (or milk-and-
   water)

Place all the dry ingredients plus the syrup in a mixing bowl and add the milk or milk-and-water. Stir and mix thoroughly to a fairly moist dough. Handle a little and drop into a well-greased 1 lb loaf tin 7 in. × 4 in. Push the dough well down, smooth the top and cover with foil. Bake for 1 hour at 450°F (Mark 8). Cool in the tin, tap the sides and turn onto a wire tray or wooden board.

Sam's Steamed Bread

A very useful recipe for campers or for those temporarily without an oven

8 oz self-raising flour
1½ cups medium oatmeal
1 tbsp brown sugar
1½ cups (approx.) milk, preferably
   sour (the thicker the better)
1 tbsp black treacle
¾ tsp bicarbonate of soda
½ tsp salt
1 teacup (or less) of sultanas

Have ready 3 or 4 straight-sided tins, greased. Mix all the dry ingredients in a bowl. Stir in the milk and treacle which have been beaten together. Turn into the prepared tins, put on the lids and steam for 2½–3 hours. Turn onto a wire rack to cool. Cut into thin slices and butter.

Note: *This bread can also be made using dates, nuts and/or spices. Cocoa tins, salt tins, etc., can be used by cutting off the top and hammering back the rough edges.*

Spring Evening Rhubarb Bread

from Gail Hatch

This bread is moist and heavy and may be used as a dessert bread. It is best on a cool Spring evening. It's nutritious as well as delicious. Makes two loaves.

12 oz wholewheat flour (or plain
   white)
2 tsps salt
6 tbsps melted butter
1 tsp cinnamon
⅔ cup powdered milk
4 tsps baking powder
12 oz sugar
About 2 cups cooked, unsweetened
   rhubarb

Mix thoroughly all the ingredients except the rhubarb, then add enough rhubarb (about 2 cups) to moisten.
   Pour into 2 loaf pans. Bake at 350°F (Mark 4) for about 40 minutes. Let cool and remove from pans onto wire rack.

Try using stewed apple, apricots, or any other suitable fruit instead of rhubarb.

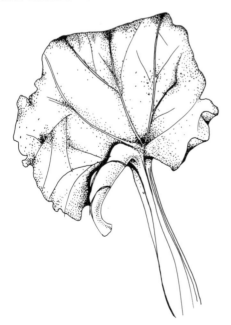

Welsh Treacle Loaf Cake

From Mrs. Booth, Wernddn Genol Farm, Altwen, Ponterdawe, Swansea

1 tbsp margarine
8 oz self-raising flour
1 tsp bicarbonate of soda, dissolved
   in 4 fluid oz milk
2 tbsps black treacle
4 oz sugar

Melt the margarine and treacle and pour onto a mixture of the flour, sugar, milk and bicarbonate of soda. Place in a square or oblong tin and bake for 35 minutes at 300°F (Mark 1–2).

Bara Brith—Fatless

An old Welsh recipe

12 oz mixed dried fruit
¾ pint of cold tea
1 egg, beaten
3 oz melted butter if required
1 lb self-raising flour
4 oz sugar
A pinch of mixed spice

Soak the dried fruit in the tea overnight. Next day, add the beaten egg to the mixture. Mix the flour, sugar and spice together, and add the fruit, tea and egg mixture to form a wettish dough, stirring with a wooden spoon. To produce a Bara Brith with a more cake-like texture, add 3 oz melted butter at this stage. Bake on a greased flat tin at 350°F (Mark 4) for 1½–2 hours.

Cool; slice and spread with butter.

Canadian Boiled Fruit Loaf

1 lb mixed dried fruit
4 oz sugar
3 oz margarine
1 tsp bicarbonate of soda
A bare ½ pint cold water
1 lb self-raising flour
½ tsp almond essence
1 egg, well beaten

Boil the fruit, sugar, margarine, bicarbonate of soda and water together, and leave overnight. Next morning add the flour, almond essence and egg. Mix well, and bake in a well-greased flat tin at 310°F (Mark 2) for 2 hours.

Dublin Tea Loaf

1 lb self-raising flour
1 egg
½ pint cold tea
8 oz sugar
8 oz currants
8 oz raisins
4 oz mixed peel
4 oz cherries (optional)

Soak the fruit in the cold tea overnight. Next day stir the fruit and mix in the flour and egg. Place in a greased tin and bake at 325°F (Mark 3) for 2 hours. If the cake browns too soon, cover it with greased paper.

Irish Treacle Bread

8 oz self-raising flour
½ tsp salt
½ tsp ground ginger
½ tsp mixed spice
2 oz margarine
3–4 tbsps milk
2 tbsps treacle
2 oz moist brown sugar
1 egg

Sieve the dry ingredients. Melt the margarine in the milk, cool slightly and add the treacle, sugar and beaten egg. Add the liquid to the dry ingredients and mix well. Pour into a greased loaf tin about 4 in. × 7 in. and bake in a moderate oven, 350°F (Mark 4) for about 1 hour.

Spicy Dripping Brack Bread

This is an easily made fruity bread, which will use up any surplus dripping

Weigh the **dripping** *and to every 6 oz add:*

3 oz dried fruit
1 lb self-raising flour
2 oz sugar
A pinch of salt
1 rounded tbsp mixed spice
1 egg, beaten
A little milk to mix
Cold tea

Cover the dried fruit with cold tea and leave to soak overnight. Next day rub the dripping into the flour and add the sugar, salt, spice, fruit and tea; mix with the beaten egg and enough milk to make a dryish mixture. Grease well two loaf tins and sprinkle with flour, or line with the wrapping paper from the butter or any other fat. Place the mixture in the tins and bake at 350°F (Mark 4) until well risen and 'set'.

Leave for a while before buttering.

Teisan Lap

A nice moist Welsh cake bread for tea, easy for a busy cook—just throw it all together and out it comes in no time.

6 oz self-raising flour
3 oz fat
3 oz sugar
3 oz currants/peel/cherries
A pinch of grated nutmeg
1 egg, beaten
Sour milk (see p. 13)
A little grated orange peel if required

Rub the fat into the flour and add the sugar, fruit and spice. Add the beaten egg to the mixture with enough sour milk to make a really loose batter. A little grated orange peel adds a tasty tang. Bake in a greased swiss-roll tin at 350°F (Mark 4) for 45–50 minutes.

Dodie Jones' Walnut Bread

Given to me in the Cambrian Inn, Solva, Pembs., one Saturday lunchtime.

4 oz granulated sugar
1 oz syrup

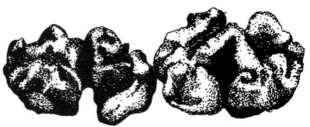

1 egg, beaten
A pinch of salt
2 oz sultanas
8 oz plain flour
2 oz walnuts, roughly chopped
3 tsps baking powder

Grease and flour a loaf tin 8½ in. × 4½ in., 2½ in. deep. Heat the sugar and syrup with the sultanas in a saucepan and stir gently until the sugar is dissolved. Allow to cool. Sift the flour, salt and baking powder into a bowl and add the roughly chopped nuts.

Tip the melted sugar mixture onto the beaten egg and then add to the dry ingredients. Stir until smooth. Pour into the prepared tin and bake at 350°F (Mark 4) for about 1½ hours. Test as for sponge cake, by finger pressure on the top—if the dent springs back, the bread is done.

Alice's Irish Brack

From Connemara

This is a very special 'brack' and strictly not for teetotallers!

1 lb sultanas
1 lb raisins
¾ pint strong black tea
3 eggs
Alcohol as required!
1 lb brown sugar
1 lb plain flour
3 tsps baking powder
Mixed spice or cinnamon if liked

Alice's instructions are brief. She says: 'Soak fruit overnight. I put in some whisky!' That's all.

In the morning, put all the dry ingredients in a bowl, pour on the soaked fruit, add the beaten eggs and mix well. Bake at 300°F (Mark 1–2) in a greased and floured tin, preferably a square one, for about 2½–3 hrs.

In 1971, with another farmer and his wife, my husband and I went to stay in Connemara. One day I was walking along the shore road, the other three having gone fishing, when I heard two men quarrelling. So belligerent did they sound that I was quite scared and ran up a bank out of sight. After a few minutes the arguers came nearer and I dared to peep out, curiosity overcoming fear. To my amazement what hove into view was one very drunk, somewhat shabby little man swerving from side to side of the lane on his old bicycle, carrying on a heated and acrimonious argument such as I have seldom heard, with himself! It was so unexpected and so funny that I laughed till I cried. The hotel owners told me he did this regularly every Friday night.

Gradually beat the sugar into the softened margarine until fluffy. Add the eggs and mix till blended. Stir in the nuts and raisins. If preferred, use part dates and a little home-candied orange peel instead of all raisins. Sift the flour with the bicarbonate of soda, nutmeg and cinnamon three times. Add, alternately with the stewed apples, to the creamed mixture, beating well after each addition (be sure the apples are stewed into a pulp before using). When blended, turn into a 1 lb greased loaf tin (8 in. × 4 in.). Bake at 350°F (Mark 4) for about 1 hour.

Apple Loaf Cake

from Devonshire

8 oz sugar
2 eggs, beaten
1 cup chopped raisins (or part dates if preferred)
¾ tsp bicarbonate of soda
1 level tsp ground cinnamon
4 oz margarine
½ cup chopped nuts
8 oz sifted plain flour
¼ tsp grated nutmeg
1 cup stewed apples

Coconut and Carrot Loaf Cake

Serves 5; use 1 large or 2 small loaf tins, greased

2 cups brown sugar
7½ fluid oz corn oil
4 eggs, beaten
2 tsps baking powder
1 cup dessicated coconut
1 large carrot, grated
1 tsp salt
1 tbsp cinnamon
8 oz wholewheat flour
1 cup chopped walnuts
1 tsp vanilla essence

Mix the sugar with the oil and beaten eggs. Blend the flour with the baking powder and salt, and add the wet ingredients to the dry ones. Fold in the spice, nuts, flavourings, coconut and carrot. Fill the ready-greased loaf tins half-full and bake at 350°F (Mark 4) for 1 hour.

Date Bread
from Warwickshire

1 lb dates, stoned and chopped
7½ fluid oz boiling water
1½ tsps bicarbonate of soda
2 oz butter
1 lb plain flour
8 oz sugar
2 eggs, beaten

Pour the boiling water over the prepared dates, dissolve the bicarbonate of soda in this and leave all to soak till cold. Rub the butter into the flour and sugar. Beat the eggs and mix all the ingredients together. Knead into 2 loaves and put into well-greased loaf tins. Bake at 325°F (Mark 3) for 1½ hours.

Date Nut Bread
from California

8 oz plain white or wholewheat flour
2 tsps baking powder
2 tsps cinnamon
½ tsp mace
2 tsps grated orange rind
2 eggs, well beaten
6 tbsps butter or margarine
½ cup brown sugar

½ cup milk
½ cup chopped walnuts
1 cup chopped dates
½ tsp salt

Grease a large loaf tin. Sift together the flour, spices, salt and baking powder. Cream the fat and sugar and beat in the eggs.

Add to the mixture the dry ingredients alternately with the milk, beginning and ending with the dry ingredients. Fold in the dates, nuts and orange rind.

Place in the greased tin and bake at 325°F (Mark 3) for 60–75 minutes. Cool in the tin for 5 minutes before turning out onto a cake rack.

Serve just as it is, or with butter. For a real treat, try it with cream cheese.

Yorkshire Spice Bread

12 oz self-raising flour
4 oz margarine or butter
4 oz sugar
2 eggs, beaten
2 tsps mixed spice
2 oz each of sultanas and currants
A little milk to mix

Mix all the ingredients together, adding the beaten eggs last of all. Mix to a smooth paste. Put into well-greased tins and bake for 1 hour at 350°F (Mark 4).

And So to Bread

'What hymns are sung, what praises said, for home-made miracles of bread?'

Untermeyer

Very few pleasures are as gratifying as the smell of your first batch of real home-made yeasted bread, and as you take up the skill where your grandmother or great-grandmother left off, you will probably marvel at how simple a process it is, and your confidence will be increased enormously. It is so easy that, with a little assistance, quite young children really enjoy making bread, or at least helping in the exercise.

In fact, bread-making is very much like raising a family—after a while, you learn to throw out the book of rules and follow your own instinct and common-sense.

In a sense, it is simply a question of 'Know Thyself'—since one bread recipe is as useful as another, just choose the one which suits you and your conditions and temperament best. So go on, enjoy yourself! There's nothing difficult or mysterious about making bread. It's perfectly easy once you get to know about yeast.

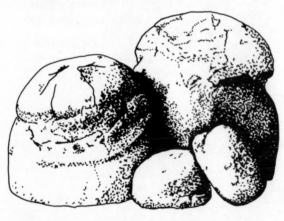

Living, Bubbling Yeast

'Know ye not that a little leaven leaveneth the whole lump?'

1 Cor. Chap 5 v. 6

There is a nice story about a slave living thousands of years ago, who made leavened bread by accident.

He left some dough in a pan and, going on with other work, completely forgot about it. Some days later, when he discovered what he had done, he was just about to throw the whole thing out when he saw his master coming up. He quickly mixed the old dough in with the new he was then making and the resulting bread was so light, so superior in every way that he was asked to explain just how he had managed to make such delicious, thoroughly acceptable bread, such a welcome change from the usual heavy old stuff. When he confessed what he had done he was promoted and was ordered to continue making bread in that fashion for the rest of his time. And so a new type of bread was born. The slave didn't know it, but one of the many wild yeasts which are carried in the air had mixed with his dough and caused it to rise.

There is every evidence that the Chinese and the Egyptians were eating leavened bread by 5000 BC, though it has not been positively established which of them first found the way to introduce yeast into their dough. Any maker of home-made wine will know that wild yeasts exist in the air, though we know little about them, and yeast was not marketed commercially in its dried—or dehydrated—form until comparatively recent years, when French and German scientists were called in to discover more about yeast in the all-important winemaking which was a valuable industry in their countries.

It is probable that neither the Chinese nor the Egyptians understood why their bread became 'leavened' in this fashion, but we now know that yeast is a living breathing plant, a mysterious substance consisting of a mass of microscopic plants, distant cousin to the mushroom, belonging to the fungus family and akin to bacteria. Each of these plants is a single cell which reproduces itself by budding. One small packet of English yeast or one American 'cake' of yeast contains millions of such cells.

The usefulness of these tiny plants is that they are able to produce fermentation in starch and sugar solutions. The chief products of this fermentation are alcohol and carbon dioxide gas. The alcohol-making properties are used in brewing and winemaking, while the gas-making properties are used in baking bread, since the carbon dioxide forms bubbles which lighten the dough by filling it with tiny round holes.

Now, once we realise that yeast is a living, breathing thing we tend to take more care of it, just as we handle a real live baby with more care and thoughtfulness than a doll.

Yeast needs food, warmth and kindness. The food we give it is usually in the form of sugar; the warmth we can vary according to how speedily we wish to finish the whole process; the kindness shows itself by the way we treat the yeast. In order to be kind to your yeast it is useful to remember that its deadly enemies are salt and heat; either of these can kill it. Until recently, many recipes advised the cook to 'prove' the yeast by mixing it in a small bowl with nothing but sugar. The newest idea, however, is that even this is too

drastic, and the kinder way to start it working is to put it in a jug together with *all* the liquid required in the recipe, and add to this mixture the sugar, honey, syrup or whatever is called for.

Yeast needs fresh air as well, so that is why we 'punch down' the dough when it has had time to be blown up by the yeast's action. This expels the gas, which would make large holes in the bread, and allows the yeast to breathe. If the carbon dioxide and the alcohols build up too much in the glutenous mixture of the dough, the yeast suffocates and dies.

When, finally, the dough is put in the oven, the yeast's work is done and the heat of the oven finishes it off—one could almost mourn for it!

When fat is added to a yeast dough, in order to make a richer mixture, it is as well to remember that fat slows down the action of the yeast, so it is necessary to increase the proportion of yeast, and a longer time should be allowed for rising.

It is very easy to buy yeast these days, yet the introduction of dried yeast in the 1960s was revolutionary, and even fresh German yeast was a novelty in early Victorian days. It is still sold fresh in some country districts and small bakeries, and in dried form it is sold by many supermarkets, grocers and multiple chemists such as Boots.

It is possible to make your own yeasts, as our forefathers did, but space does not permit any details here.

What you will Need for Making Bread with Yeast

Basic Ingredients

Flour (plain)
Salt
Fat or Oil (optional)
Yeast
Sugar
Water

Basic Equipment

A very large bowl
A large jug
A half-pint measure
A small saucepan
A knife, tablespoon and dessertspoon
A strong wooden spoon or spatula (for the batter-method dough)
A working surface
Bread tins—four 1 lb, or two 2 lb
A hot oven

About the Ingredients

Flour

Only plain flour (that is, not self-raising), may be used with yeast, but apart from this rule any chosen flour, or mixture of two or more flours, is suitable. Some flours are better for breadmaking, such as the 'hard' or 'strong' flours imported from Canada, etc. See p. 11. Many home bakers mix plain white flour with wheatmeal or wholemeal to please their families; others use nothing but wholemeal flour.

Salt

Salt is added to give flavour to the bread. Salt is a 'killer' of yeast; they should never meet directly. To avoid any chance of this, take a little of the water used in the recipe to dissolve the salt separately. This mixture may then be added to the flour before you add the yeasty mixture.

Fat or Oil

Many of the older recipes advocate rubbing the fat into the warmed flour, but in practice it seems that a better texture is obtained in the finished bread if the fat is melted; this has become evident since cooking oil came into popular usage. Any fat may be used—lard, butter, margarine or dripping. To save washing up, simply put the water in which the salt has been dissolved into a small saucepan, add the fat and melt gently. Allow it to cool slightly, make a 'well' in the flour with the back of your hand, and pour in the mixture. Fat is not strictly necessary but the bread will have a better keeping quality and will be moister.

Yeast

Dried yeast or fresh (baker's) yeast are equally effective for your purpose. Dried yeast comes in tins or 1 oz sachets and will keep, if properly stored, for up to nine months. Best results are obtained by **sprinkling the dried yeast onto the liquid** and sugar mixture and whisking briskly with a fork. Fresh or baker's yeast is not sold in many places but may be found more often in rural areas, where the demand is perhaps greater. To test fresh yeast make sure that: (**a**) it smells 'sweet'; (**b**) it is firm and crumbly; (**c**) it is fawn in colour; and (**d**) when a few 'crumbs' are mixed with a little sugar, the yeast turns to a creamy consistency. Best results are obtained by **pouring the water and sugar mixture onto the fresh yeast.**

Bakers' shops or small grocery shops are quite used to being asked for 2 oz yeast at a time, but fresh yeast will keep for a while in the deep freeze—if you pack it in small cartons in the exact quantity required for use, it is a simple matter to thaw and use it. Remember that heat kills yeast, so thaw gently!

Sugar

The sugar is needed to feed the yeast, so if brown sugar is preferred to white, or honey or syrup to either, the effect is the same. Until quite recently the custom was to 'prove' the yeast by mixing the sugar directly with it until the yeast was 'creamed'. Modern thought, however, is that this method is too drastic for the yeast and tends to weaken it; most people now seem to mix all the liquid with the sugar—or whatever—and add this to the yeast as described on p. 46.

Water

Perhaps the whole operation depends on the accuracy with which the water is measured. At first, use only the quantity specified in the recipe—if more is needed, add it little by little. If the dough is too wet, the bread will be heavy; if it is too dry, the bread will be crumbly. The temperature of the water is also very important—the word 'tepid' is frequently used to denote the required temperature, but this leaves room for mistakes. A simple but absolutely safe way to get the water just right for the yeast is by putting one pint of cold with half a pint of boiling water and using right away. Quickly add the sugar and then add the whole mixture to the yeast if fresh yeast is used, or sprinkle the yeast on top of the mixture if dried yeast is used. A quick stir with a fork, and then this vital part of the yeasted breadmaking process can be put aside in a warm place to 'rise'.

About the Equipment

It is most helpful to keep all your equipment close at hand—not stuck on a shelf about 8 feet up!

Bowl

The bowl needs to be very large because not only does flour tend to fly everywhere, but room is needed for the dough to rise and expand. A plastic washing-up bowl kept for the purpose is good but a preserving pan, very big mixing bowl, outsized saucepan, or anything similar you have in the home will do, providing there

is sufficient room to mix the dough and subsequently to allow it to rise. It is possible to manage without a bowl at all by pouring the flour directly onto a board and mixing the liquid and yeast straight into a 'well' in the middle. If you know yourself to be a neat-handed person then this method is fine for you, but many of us are anything but neat and tidy and so we use bowls for safety. When planning which bowl to use, take into account what facilities you have for warming the bowl and the flour, and for keeping the dough out of draughts, and judge accordingly. If your warming space is limited try using a small plastic bucket instead of a bowl—it will fit in any corner.

Jug

The ideal jug for breadmaking is a see-through type large enough to hold all the liquid at once, plus allowing space for the yeast to rise. Thus the fermentation or rising process may be kept under observation. Most of us have had an overflow of frothing yeast in our time! A large bowl may be used instead but a jug is easier for pouring.

Half-pint Measure

Remember that the success of the bread greatly depends on the accurate measuring of the water. If no graduated jug is available, you may still have an ever-ready measure at hand, for many of the modern coffee mugs hold exactly half a pint. A glass beer mug is accurate but not practical because boiling water has to be measured as well as cold.

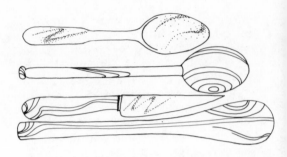

Small Saucepan

This will be needed if the fat is to be melted but, to save on washing up, use the same saucepan for dissolving the salt (in a little of the cold water).

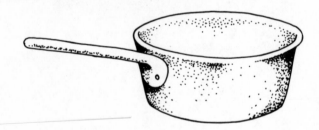

Knife, Spoons and/or Spatula

A knife will be needed, large enough to cut through the dough for dividing it into loaves. A dessertspoon (old-fashioned pudding spoon) and a tablespoon are also very useful. For making bread the batter-method way, a strong wooden spoon or spatula is helpful, but in all breadmaking hands are as good a tool as any!

Working Surface

It is possible to do the whole operation in the one big bowl, mixing, kneading and all, but the bread will be far better in texture for being kneaded on a flat surface, as the dough can then be stretched and the gluten spread through more evenly. Any easily cleaned surface is suitable as long as it is smooth, especially if it is wood —it is disconcerting to find a splinter in the loaf! As long as the surface is large enough to give you room to handle the dough, say a minimum of 18 in. square, you will manage, but ideally the more space the better.

Bread Tins

Bread can be, and frequently is, baked without tins at all, but at first, tins are useful for keeping the dough in good shape. Cake tins may be used, but for best results proper bread tins kept for the purpose are ideal. When buying them, if possible choose those with rounded corners, as these are most easily cleaned. The way to avoid the loaves sticking to the tin is to start as you mean to go on—NEVER WASHING THE TINS. Instead, wipe them out while still hot with a greased cloth or paper. To prepare the tins for the dough, they should be warmed and greased (any fat will do). When the dough is placed in

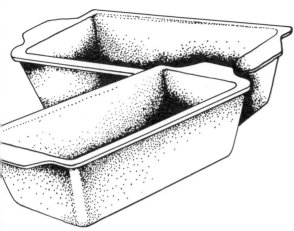

be warm enough to allow the dough to rise to double its size within 40–50 minutes— that is, if you want to make the bread as quickly as is reasonable. Since dough must not be exposed to direct heat until it is actually ready for the oven, a good place for many people in these modern days is a cosy corner in the airing cupboard. Simply put bowl and all in a large plastic bag, secure with a wire tie and leave until ready.

Terminology You May Hear Used

'Knocking Back'—this simply means what it says! The dough has to be knocked back at some stage in order to let out the gases which have built up in it. All you have to do is use your fist to punch it back after it has 'got above itself' before going on to the next stage.

'Proving'—this term means to test the yeast's rising power. In the days when all yeasts were home-made it was necessary to 'prove' it before risking it in the huge quantities of flour they used in those days. Even in these days, if the yeast does not froth as required you will know it has lost its rising power—but give it a bit of time, it may be that it is cold or needs a little more sugar.

About Using Yeast

Regular bread-makers buy fresh yeast in bulk, 1 lb at a time, from a bakery or baker's shop. They store it in the refrigerator by keeping it in the waxed or grease-proof paper in which it was wrapped, inside *a complete covering of aluminium foil*— the secret is that the foil *must* completely cover the package. The yeast comes in a block, like a lump of cheese or slabcake, and may be used as required. Yeast is not the most expensive ingredient in the recipe but you may as well use it as economically as possible, so at first use only the amount stated in the recipe. The only virtue in using a lot of yeast is that the bread-making is speeded up, but the flavour of the bread may be too yeasty for some palates.

the tin, before the second rising, it should come half-way up the sides. Any higher and it will spill over the top when fully risen.

Hot Oven

Bread may be steamed and it is also possible to cook yeasted bread on a bake-stone or griddle, but oven-cooked bread is crisper and crustier. Oven temperatures are given in the recipes, but you should get to know your own oven and adjust the temperatures accordingly if necessary. *It is a safe rule to start cooking bread in a hot oven and then to reduce the temperature.* In the case of solid fuel or oil-fired cookers, follow the manufacturer's instructions, but generally this means starting the bread in the middle of the hot oven and finishing it off on the 'floor' of that oven; or, if a two-oven model, the finishing-off may be completed in the slower oven. If using gas or electric stoves, it is always best to follow the manufacturer's advice.

Notes to Help you with your Bread-making

Where to Put your Bread to Rise

The spot you choose for putting the covered bowl of dough to rise must be out of all draughts. Apart from that, it should

Making Bread in an Electric Mixer

This is bread-making made very easy! This labour-saving machine will save time as well as energy, but there are certain tips which may help.

In winter, always warm the bowl and beaters. If you forget to put them in a warm place, a last-minute warming in boiling water will do the trick.

In making batter breads, use the beater for the first operation of beating the batter, and then the dough hook after adding the second half of flour, for the kneading.

Important: About Flour

The 'dampness' of flour varies from season to season, according to the weather influences during the growing period and harvesting of the wheat plants.

Always use the recommended proportions of liquid to start with, but if the dough seems too crumbly and does not bind together in one nice smooth ball, add extra water sparingly until you can feel that the texture is correct.

Deep-freezing Home-made Bread

The bread must be absolutely cold before it is put in a plastic bag. It is very helpful to add a label, showing the date and type of bread, for future reference.

Thawing out Home-made Bread

Allow as much time as possible for this process to achieve the best results; the crust can be re-crisped by popping the loaf into a hot oven for a few minutes after thawing. If you are caught on the hop by unexpected demands, simply put the bread into a warm oven for as long as it takes to unfreeze, covering it with foil to prevent burning.

A Note on Kneading

The object of kneading is to stretch the dough in order to spread the yeast and gluten evenly throughout it. The second

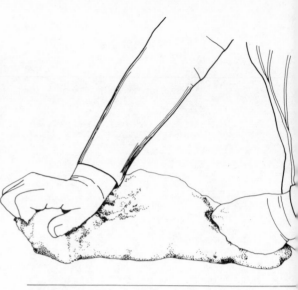

Kneading the dough—enjoy yourself!

kneading, after the dough has doubled in size, has the additional object of 'knocking back' the dough in order to let out the gases which have built up in it.

There is no 'correct' way to knead; simply pull, punch, twist and stretch the dough in all directions until it is smooth and soft and leaves the sides of the bowl cleanly. It's a wonderful way to work off frustrations!

Quantities

A 2 lb loaf (total weight) is what we usually think of as a large loaf; a 1 lb loaf, a small one.

A recipe using 1 lb of flour will make approximately 10–12 large rolls.

Tips and Tricks-of-the-Trade

- First read your recipe
- Remember to switch on the oven
- Warm the mixing bowl and flour before you start
- If the bread sounds hollow when tapped on the bottom, it's cooked
- If you like your bread crisp, take it out of the tins for the last ten minutes of cooking time and cook bottoms up

Basic Recipe for Bread in 5 Easy Stages

This timetable will give you bread in time for 5 o'clock tea; adjust it to any time of day to suit you. The recipe will make four 1 lb loaves.

3 lb flour (warmed)
1 oz salt
2 oz fresh yeast *or* 1 oz dried yeast

2 level tsps honey *or* sugar *or* syrup
$1\frac{1}{2}$ pints tepid water (1 pint boiling, $\frac{1}{2}$ pint cold)

Stage 1 1.30 pm

- Into a large jug or bowl put the sugar and tepid water; then add the yeast (if dried yeast, sprinkle on the liquid; if fresh, pour liquid on yeast). Stir with a fork and leave to froth.
- Put the flour into a large warm bowl and add the salt. It is best to dissolve the salt first in a little of the water. Mix with a fork; make a 'well'.
- Give an extra stir to the yeast mixture in the jug to ensure that all the yeast is dissolved, then pour into the well in the flour. Mix with a fork or wooden spoon.
- When all the flour is incorporated, knead the mixture in the bowl for about 5 minutes, turning the bowl round, until the dough is smooth and soft and leaves the edges of the bowl cleanly.

Stage 2 Approx. 2.00 pm

- Leave the dough in the bowl, covered with a cloth or large plastic bag, until it has doubled in size. This will take 30–50 minutes in most kitchens. The bread-making programme can be easily interrupted and postponed at this point; see p. 52.

Stage 3 Approx. 2.40 pm

- When the dough has doubled, turn it onto a lightly floured board and knead again, for at least 10 minutes, in the manner best suited to yourself, but trying to stretch the dough while mixing and kneading it in order to spread the yeast and the gluten evenly through the dough.
- Divide the dough into 4 equal pieces, each weighing about 1 lb, and press into suitably prepared tins (warmed and greased). Cover with a cloth, put out of draughts, and leave to double again, in the tins (about 35 minutes). Don't leave overlong at this stage.

Stage 4 Approx. 3.30 pm

- Cook in a hot oven (425°F, Mark 7) for about 35 minutes.

Stage 5 Approx. 4.05 pm

- When you think it is cooked, tap the bottom of the loaves; the bread should sound hollow. Remove from the oven and cool on a rack.

Alternative Programme

In Stage 2, it was mentioned that the timetable could be varied as required. This is where you have the opportunity of putting the dough away for a while, if wished.

Depending on where you leave the dough to rise, this break in operation may take 1 hour in a cool room, 3-4 hours in a cold larder or 12 hours in the fridge.

It is even possible to put the dough away in the deep freeze until required. The big manufacturers of bread do this, and sell the product as ready-to-bake bread.

When you wish to resume your bread-making, simply take the frozen or refrigerated dough into the kitchen until it is warm and pliable enough to knead. Proceed to Stage 3 by kneading for at least 10 minutes.

Mrs. Griffiths' Brown Bread

From Tresais, Caerfarchell, Dyfed
Makes four to five 1 lb loaves

3 lb plain flour (white)
A pinch of salt
1¾ pints tepid water
1 tsp sugar
4 oz brown flour
1 oz very fresh yeast *or* ½ oz dried
  yeast

Mix the yeast with the sugar and a little of the water and add to the flour and salt in a bowl, with enough tepid water to make a pliable dough. Cover and leave in a warm place for ½-¾ hour. When well risen, place in 4-5 tins and leave to rise again for another 20 minutes. Cook for 20 minutes at 425°F (Mark 7), then lower the temperature to 400°F (Mark 6) and leave for a further 25-30 minutes.

Gluten-free Bread for Special Diets

Makes two 1 lb loaves

12 oz Nutregen Wheat Starch
1 tsp salt
1 tsp sugar
1 oz cooking fat
1 oz fresh yeast
8 fluid oz cold milk mixed with
  4 fluid oz-boiling water

Sift together the wheat starch and salt, and rub in the fat. Cream the sugar and yeast together, with a little of the milk and water mixture; then add this liquid to the rest of the milk and water. Make a well in the centre of the wheat starch mixture and pour in the liquid. Mix and knead until smooth; cover the bowl with a cloth or large plastic bag and leave to rise in the warm for 20 minutes, until risen and spongy.

Knead again, and then divide into two. Place each half in a well-greased 1 lb loaf tin, cover, and leave in the warm for a further 20 minutes until the dough has nearly filled the tins. Place in a pre-heated oven at 425°F (Mark 7) and bake for 20 minutes. Turn out onto a wire rack.

Replace the wire rack in the oven until the loaves are lightly coloured—according to the oven, this may take from 5 to 20 minutes. Do not overbake, or the starch will crystallise and become crumbly in texture.

Note: A large egg may be used instead of 2 fl. oz of the cold milk if a richer gluten-free loaf is required. This egg should be beaten up with the rest of the milk before you add the boiling water. The rest of the recipe remains the same.

The loaf can be kept for long periods if it is sliced and 'rusked' in a low oven (300°F, Mark 2) until golden brown.

Different Shapes for Bread and Rolls

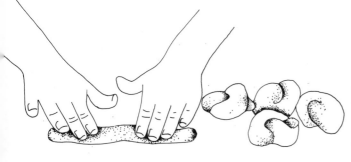

Knot (for rolls)

1. With your hands roll the dough into a sausage shape (approx. 6 in. long) on the working surface.
2. Tie into a knot.

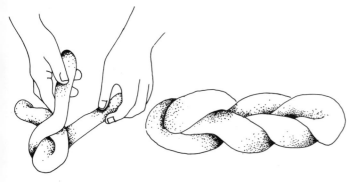

Plait

1. Divide the dough into three equal pieces.
2. Roll each piece into a sausage shape (approx. 12–14 in. long for a 1 lb loaf).
3. Pinch the three pieces together at one end.
4. Plait.
5. Pinch the pieces together at the other end. Brush the ends with beaten egg to secure.

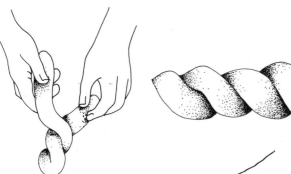

Twist

1. Divide the dough into two equal pieces.
2. Roll each piece into a long sausage shape.
3. Pinch the pieces together at one end.
4. Twist.
5. Pinch the pieces together at the other end. Brush the ends with beaten egg to secure.

Cottage

1. Cut the dough into two pieces representing one-third and two-thirds of the total.
2. Roll each piece into a ball.
3. Dampen the bottom of the small ball and place it on top of the large one.
4. Push down in the middle as far as you can with a floured finger, to secure.

Batter Breads

Batter bread is a very quick, easy way of making basic bread. It can be made as easily by hand as by electric mixer, by old and young, and once you have the hang of it, no instructions will be necessary— you will know the texture of the dough by the feel of it.

The reason for choosing Elizabeth's recipe for wholemeal bread was that it is such an easy one, so quick and convenient in every way, that it makes a good recipe for beginners.

Elizabeth's Wholemeal Bread

As made by Elizabeth Haines, the well-known artist from Preceli Mountains, Pembrokeshire. This is a very quick, no-messing-about recipe; to save time, leave the flour in a warm spot overnight.

3 lb wholemeal flour, warmed
3 tsps dried yeast
1½ pints tepid water. (½ pint boiling, 1 pint cold)—more if needed
1 tbsp brown sugar
1 tbsp coarse salt

Makes two 1 lb loaves and 20 rolls

While the yeast is dissolving in half the tepid water, mix half the flour, the brown sugar and the salt in a warmed basin. To this, add the rest of the warm water, mixing it all into a batter; then add the dissolved yeast, mix it in, and leave in a warm place, covered, with a damp cloth, for 15 minutes.

Beat the remaining flour into the mixture and knead for 5 or 10 minutes until the dough is firm and does not stick to your hands. Be patient— it will suddenly happen. Cut the dough into 4 sections and place 2 of them in warm greased bread tins. For rolls, cut the remaining dough into 20 pieces, roll each one quickly into a ball, and place on a greased baking tray. Leave the dough to rise in a warm place until it has doubled in size.

Place the rolls above the loaves in the oven and bake at 425°F (Mark 7) for about 45 minutes, removing the rolls after 15–20 minutes.

Quick White Batter Bread

3 lb plain flour
1 level tsp sugar
¼ pint boiling milk
1¼ pints cold water
1 tsp sugar, honey *or* syrup
1½ oz fresh yeast (or ¾ oz dried yeast)
4 level tsps salt

Makes four to five 1 lb loaves

Take 1 lb of the flour and the teaspoon of sugar and put them in a bowl. Make a batter by mixing together the boiling milk, cold water, and the honey, sugar or syrup in a jug or saucepan and add the yeast; stir well, and then add all this liquid to the flour and sugar in the bowl. Beat well with a wooden spoon to a smooth batter.

Stand in a warm place for 15 minutes, covered with a cloth. This period counts as the first rising.

Next, sieve the salt into the remaining flour and add to the batter a little at a time, using the wooden spoon at first, and then, as the batter becomes more doughy, finishing off with your hands. Knead well until the dough feels elastic (about 5–10 minutes).

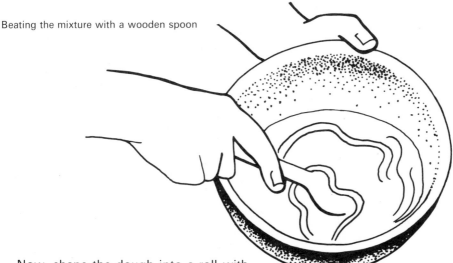

Beating the mixture with a wooden spoon

Now, shape the dough into a roll with floured hands; cut into 4 or 5 equal pieces, take each piece in turn and flatten it on the board, then press out and roll up like a Swiss roll. Do this two or three times to each piece, then place in well-greased and floured tins, flatten into the tins with the back of the hand and press into the corners. Cover the tins with a cloth and leave in a warm place (i.e. out of draughts but not near heat) to double in size. This will take about 30–35 minutes.

Bake at 425°F (Mark 7) for 35 minutes; or 475°F (Mark 9) for 10 minutes, then 400°F (Mark 6) for a further 20 minutes. If bigger 2 lb loaves are made, leave it in the oven for a further 10–15 minutes.

Watchtower Bread

From Caroline Roach (calling on behalf of Jehovah's Witness). A quick and easy 'no knead' batter bread. Makes two 2 lb loaves.

1 tsp treacle
1 tsp salt
$\frac{1}{2}$ oz butter or oil
$\frac{1}{2}$ pint very hot water
1 fluid oz warm water
$\frac{1}{2}$ pint cold water
$\frac{3}{4}$ oz fresh yeast (or $\frac{3}{8}$ oz dried yeast)
$\frac{1}{2}$ tsp sugar
$1\frac{3}{4}$ lb plain flour—wholemeal, *or* wheatmeal *or* half brown and half white

Mix the treacle, salt and butter or oil with the hot water. Add the cold water to this mixture and gradually add $\frac{1}{2}$ lb of the flour. Cream the yeast and sugar with the warm water, and allow to foam. Add to the mixture.

Gradually stir in a further 1–$1\frac{1}{4}$ lb flour until the mixture is quite stiff.

Put into 2 well-greased 2 lb loaf tins and leave to rise in a warm place. Heat oven to 475°F (Mark 9), and put in loaves when risen. Reduce heat to 400°F, Mark 6 for three-quarters of an hour; turn round and bake for a further half-hour. Turn out and cool.

This recipe was given to me by a young girl who calls on behalf of the Jehovah's Witnesses. It was a freezing cold day, and as we live in a remote area I asked her in and gave her a cup of coffee for her trouble in calling. We talked only of bread (and avoided all controversial subjects!) and she gave me this delicious and trouble-free recipe.

Rubbing-In Method Bread

Rubbing-in is a very relaxing operation, much enjoyed by some cooks. Here are some recipes for these folk to try, in which the fat and/or the yeast are rubbed into the flour.

Quick Wheatmeal Bread— Rubbing-in Yeast Method

1 lb wheatmeal flour, warmed
1 lb plain white flour, warmed
2 level tsps salt
1 oz fresh yeast *or* $\frac{1}{2}$ oz dried yeast
1 pint lukewarm water ($\frac{1}{4}$ pint boiling, $\frac{3}{4}$ pint cold)
2 level tsps sugar

Makes four 1 lb loaves

Method for Fresh Yeast

Grease 4 tins and put them in a warm place. Rub yeast, flour and sugar together in a large warm bowl. Dissolve the salt in the water, and add this liquid all at once to the flour mixture; mix to a soft dough, using hand or wooden spoon.

Knead until the dough leaves the sides of the bowl cleanly. (If necessary, use a little extra flour here—but only a little at a time! Too much spoils the bread.)

Half-fill the well-greased warm tins with dough and flatten in the tins with the back of the hand. Cover with a cloth, and allow to rise in a warm place for 45–60 minutes, or longer in a cooler place, until the dough has doubled in size.

Remove the cloth and bake on the middle shelf of a hot oven (425°F, Mark 7) for 35–40 minutes.

Method for Dried Yeast

Add a teaspoonful of sugar to the lukewarm water; when dissolved, sprinkle the dried yeast on top and whisk well with a fork. Leave till frothy—about 10 minutes. Then add to the flours, salt and the other sugar and mix to a dough as above. In order to mix the dough thoroughly with the yeast, turn the dough onto a floured board and knead it well with all your might until the dough is smooth and silky. Then continue to fill the tins and cook as above.

Wholewheat Bread with Fat

3 lb plain wholewheat flour
2 level tbsps sugar, honey or syrup
1$\frac{1}{2}$ pints warm water (110°F)
1 oz dried yeast *or* 2 oz fresh yeast
1 oz fat (butter, vegetable fat or oil)
1 level tbsp salt

Makes four 1 lb loaves

Grease four 1 lb loaf tins, and put in a warm place. Place the flour in a warm mixing bowl, and put it in a warm place. Dissolve 1 teaspoon of the sugar in $\frac{1}{4}$ pint of the warm water. Whisk in the dried yeast with a fork (or, if using fresh yeast, pour the liquid onto the yeast) and leave until frothy—approximately 10 minutes. Rub the fat into the flour. If using oil, do not use at this stage but add to the dough when it is partially mixed.

Dissolve the salt and remaining sugar in the remaining warm water; add this and the yeast solution to the flour. Mix thoroughly to form a smooth dough. Working quickly to keep the dough warm, knead on a floured board till it is no longer sticky. Cover the dough with a cloth, and leave in a warm place until it has doubled in size.

When the dough has risen, turn it onto a floured board and knead until firm. Divide the dough into 4 equal pieces and put them into the warm, greased tins. Cover the tins with a cloth and leave in a warm place until the dough rises approximately $\frac{1}{2}$ in. above the top of the tins. Bake at 450°F (Mark 8) for 35–40 minutes.

Plank Breads

Traditionally this bread should be cooked on a plank; however, a greased thick cast-iron frying pan, on not too great heat, would do.

Plank Bread

2 lb flour
1 tsp sugar
1 oz fresh yeast *or* $\frac{1}{2}$ oz dried yeast
1 tsp salt
1 oz lard
$\frac{1}{2}$ pint tepid milk or water

Put the flour in a warmed bowl. Put the yeast and sugar in a basin and mix with the milk or water. Mix to a dough. Cover to keep warm and leave to rise for 1 hour. Cut in 4; knead and form round flat cakes 1–1$\frac{1}{2}$ in. thick. Leave to rise for 10–15 minutes. Place on a plank or frying pan and bake one side at a time, 10 minutes each side.

These cakes can be split in half, buttered and eaten hot or cold.

Welsh Muffins

From Mrs. E. O. James, wife of the former Principal of Gelli Aur Agricultural College, Golden Grove, Carmarthen.

12 oz plain flour
12 oz strong flour
$\frac{3}{4}$ oz fresh yeast *or* $\frac{3}{8}$ oz dried yeast
1 tsp sugar
1 level tsp salt
1 oz lard
$\frac{3}{4}$ pint tepid water

Warm the flour in a bowl to hand heat. Add the salt and rub in the lard. Cream the yeast with the sugar. Make a well in the centre of the flour mixture and pour in the tepid water. Before starting to mix the flour, add the creamed yeast to the mixture, then gradually mix in the flour until a doughy consistency is obtained.

Knead well, using a little extra flour to prevent the hands sticking to the dough. After a few minutes the dough should be fine and free from the sides of the bowl. Cover with a warm cloth and set in a warm place to rise to double its size—this should take about 45 minutes.

When it is ready, turn it out onto a lightly floured pastry board and divide into 8 portions. Work each portion into a round a little over 1 in. thick and about 5–6 in. in diameter.

Allow these to rise on the pastry board in a warm place covered by a cloth (about 15 minutes). Heat a bakestone or griddle and grease it lightly. Place the muffins gently on it and cook slowly for about 15 minutes on each side. When cooked, the muffins will have a hollow sound when tapped with a knife.

The muffins can be split or sliced and buttered, after they have been allowed to cool.

Sweet and Appealing Breads

So many of us are sweet-toothed mortals that these recipes should encourage you to try something a little different. The resulting loaves will disappear before your very eyes like snow before the sun. However, they freeze well, and so can be made well ahead of schedule.

Coconut Bread

Very popular in the 18th century

1½ lb strong white flour
½ level tbsp salt
¾ pint lukewarm milk and water
2 tsps sugar
½ oz dried yeast
3–4 oz dessicated coconut *or* ½ fresh
    coconut, grated finely

Put the coconut into the milk and water, and simmer gently, being careful not to let it boil, until the liquid takes on the flavour of the coconut. Allow it to cool to lukewarm, then add the yeast and sugar and allow to froth.

Mix the salt in the flour and make a well in the centre. Pour the yeast and coconut mixture into this well and stir together thoroughly. Knead the dough well for about 10 minutes until it becomes elastic. Leave the dough in the bowl, cover with a cloth or plastic bag and put it in a warm place to rise.

When it is double its orginal size 'knock back' by punching with the fist or knead briefly again. Then divide the dough into 2 and place in well-greased warm 1 lb bread tins, pressing well down and only half-filling each tin. Cover again, and leave to rise a second time until the loaves fill the tins. Bake at 450°F (Mark 8) for the first 15 minutes, then lower the heat to 375°F (Mark 5) for another 45 minutes (approx.).

Sweet Curranty Bread

1½ lb white flour
4 oz sugar
A pinch of salt
1 oz fresh yeast *or* ½ oz dried yeast
4 oz butter, warmed
½ pint warm milk
8 oz mixed dried fruit
2 oz chopped mixed peel

Mix the flour, sugar and salt, and add the yeast creamed with a little sugar. Work in the warm butter and milk, knead, and leave to double in size, covered with a cloth, in a warm place, for approximately 1½ hours. Knead in the fruit and peel, and shape into 2 loaves or 18–20 buns; leave to rise for another 45 minutes.

Bake at 375°F (Mark 5) for 45 minutes, turning after 20 minutes. Small buns will need about 20 minutes cooking time. Cool on a wire tray and glaze with a mixture of milk and sugar.

Windfall Apple Bread

1½ lb windfalls *or* 1 lb 'good'
    cooking apples
Sugar to taste
2 lb flour, warmed
2 oz fresh yeast *or* 1 oz dried yeast
2½ fluid oz water

Place the flour in a large bowl and put to warm. Peel, core and slice the apples. Place in a saucepan with the water and sugar to taste (depending on the tartness of the apples) and stew until cooked. When cooled, strain off half a cup of the liquid from the apples. Into this whisk the yeast, and leave to froth. Allow the apples to cool a little more, then combine the warm pulp with the flour. Add the yeast mixture and mix thoroughly.

Knead well; cover with a cloth or plastic bag and leave in a warm place to rise for 3–4 hours. Shape the dough and half-fill 3 greased 1 lb loaf tins. Cover and leave to rise in the warm until doubled in size (about 45 minutes). Bake at 350°F (Mark 4) for 1–1¼ hours.

Sally Lunn Bread

An 18th century English bread

1 oz fresh yeast *or* ½ oz dried yeast
½ cup warm water (nice and warm to the fingers, but not hot)
2 tsps salt
1 lb 10 oz plain flour
Butter or margarine
2 oz sugar
3 large eggs (leave them out overnight, so they are at room temperature)
1½ cups boiled milk, cooled to lukewarm
1 cup (bare) of lard or Spry, melted

Soak the yeast in the warm water with 1 tablespoon of sugar. Beat in the eggs and the rest of the sugar. Add the cooled milk, then gradually stir in 1 lb of the flour and beat until the batter falls in sheets from the spoon. Add the melted fat, cooled. Stir in the salt and remaining flour, scraping down the bowl to incorporate all the bits on the sides. Put a little oil on top of the dough to prevent it from getting crusted, then cover and stand in a warm corner until doubled in size (about 1 hour). Punch down the dough with the fist, then cover and allow it to rest for 10 minutes.

Divide the dough in two. Butter two 8½ in. jelly ring moulds or Sally Lunn or Turks Head moulds and sprinkle with sugar and cinnamon to coat the sides. Place one half of the dough in each, cover and set to rise in a warm place for ¾ hour or until the dough has doubled in size. Bake for 1 hour at 350°F (Mark 4) or until done. Serve hot with butter if desired.

For a change, sprinkle with carraway seed or toasted sesame seed. To toast the sesame seed, simply spread it on a baking tray or shallow dish and heat it in a moderate oven (350°F) for about 20 minutes, stirring once or twice to keep the seed evenly toasted.

Bara Brith—Welsh 'Speckled' Bread

12 oz mixed dried fruit
4 oz mixed peel
½ tsp mixed spice
8 oz lard
2 lb flour—half oat, half wheat
1 pint hot water
A pinch of salt
8 oz brown or demerara sugar
2 oz fresh yeast *or* 1 oz dried yeast
2 eggs, beaten
A little oatmeal

Put the fruit, peel and spice in a 2 lb Kilner jar (or similar). Add about 1 pint of hot water and put in a warm place for the fruit to swell. Rub the fat into the flour and add salt, sugar, yeast, soaked fruit and eggs; use the spicy water to mix (you may not need it all). Knead well and shape into round flat loaves (2–4). Leave to rise for 30 minutes; brush the tops with sugared water and sprinkle with oatmeal. Bake at 300°F (Mark 1–2) for about 2 hours. When it's done it should sound hollow when the bottom is tapped.

Some enterprising country folk are buying raw grain from local farmers or corn merchants, and grinding it in their coffee grinders. Barley, oats or wheat may be used in this fashion.

Tangy and Tasty Breads

These breads appeal particularly to men, and you will notice that one of them was given to me by a farming friend who makes it for his teenage family.

Try these breads out on that evening when all the family are at home.

Cheese Bread

1 lb flour
A pinch of salt
½ oz butter
1 oz sugar
¼ pint tepid milk and water
1 oz fresh yeast *or* ½ oz dried yeast
4 oz Cheddar cheese, grated

Melt the butter and add it together with the sugar and yeast to the tepid milk and water. Mix the grated cheese and salt with the flour and make a well in the centre. Pour the yeast mixture into the well and mix thoroughly. Knead for about 10 minutes. Put the dough in a greased bowl, cover with a cloth or plastic bag and leave in a warm place until it has risen to double its original size.

Knead again, then put the dough into a well-greased tin, pressing well down, so that it half-fills the tin. Cover again and leave in a warm place until it is well risen. Bake at 375°F (Mark 5) for approximately 50 minutes. Test by tapping.

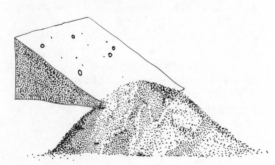

Herb and Onion Bread

Here is a recipe for Herb and Onion Bread from Neil Edmondson, Abergavenny, Mon. This goes down very well with us, eaten warm for supper with cheese, he says. The only drawback is that it disappears at one sitting. I think the smell of the herbs puts an edge on one's appetite.

10 oz wholemeal flour
½ small onion, finely chopped
½ tsp dried dill
1 tsp dried rosemary, crushed
6 tbsps milk
6 tbsps warm water
1 tbsp butter
¼ oz dried yeast
1½ oz sugar
1 tsp salt

Scald the milk and dissolve the sugar, salt and butter in it. Cool till lukewarm. In a mixing bowl, dissolve the yeast in the warm water. Add the cooled milk, flour, onion and herbs and stir well until the dough is smooth. Let the dough rise in a covered bowl for about 45–50 minutes until triple in bulk. Knock back, beat vigorously for a few minutes and turn into a greased 1 lb loaf tin. Let stand for about 10–15 minutes in a warm place before baking at 350°F (Mark 4) for 1 hour.

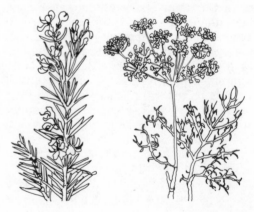

Bread Rolls, Cornish Splits and Teacakes

Many counties, it seems, have traditional recipes which have been handed down through the ages. These small breads are ideal for a variety of social occasions; many ambitious cooks prepare, for example, a wedding breakfast, a Golden Wedding celebration, or a christening party, for which these individual breads are ideal, since they can be used as a base for savoury or sweet additions.

These small breads are great fun to make and, once tasted, will undoubtedly become firm family favourites.

Cornish Splits

1 oz fresh yeast *or* ½ oz dried yeast
1 tsp sugar
1 lb plain flour
A walnut-sized piece of lard
1 tsp salt
⅓ pint of milk-and-water

Cream together yeast and sugar, and leave to foam. Put flour to warm during this process. Rub the fat into the flour and add the salt. Make a well in the centre of the flour and add the risen yeast mixture and the liquid. Mix with your hand to a dough. 'Pinch' out 24 pieces to form the splits. Brush the tops with milky water and put in a warm place to double in size. Bake at 425°F (Mark 7) till golden-brown (approximately 5–10 minutes).

Cool, then split and serve with jam or honey and clotted cream.

Dinner Rolls

These are easy to make and any surplus rolls may be stored in the deep freeze until required; then, simply re-heat in a quick oven for a few minutes. Rolls may be made from the basic bread recipe or from the following recipe. Timing and cooking are the same for either recipe. In any case, they are delicious and most acceptable.

1 lb flour, warmed
2 tsps salt
2 oz butter, lard or margarine
1 tsp sugar
½ pint milk, warmed
½ oz dried yeast *or* 1 oz fresh yeast

Rub the fat into the flour and salt. Whisk the yeast into the warm milk and add the sugar. Leave to froth. Make a well in the centre of the flour mixture and add the frothy yeast liquid. Mix to a dough, cover with a cloth or plastic bag, and place in a warm situation to double in size.

When risen, knead again; then divide into 16 even pieces and shape into small round buns by pressing in the palm of the hand on a floured board. Put to rise again on a greased baking tray covered with a cloth, in a corner away from draughts, until they are once more doubled in size (about 15 minutes).

Bake on a shelf about three-quarters of the way up the oven at 425°F (Mark 7) for 15 minutes; or 450°F (Mark 8) for 5 minutes, then at 375°F (Mark 5) for 10 minutes. Glaze with milk, or an egg and milk wash, and return to the oven to dry off for 1 minute.

Onion Bread Rolls

1 lb plain flour
½ pint tepid water
1 level tsp sugar
1 packet French onion soup
1 oz fresh yeast *or* ½ oz dried yeast
2 tbsps corn oil

Mix the yeast and sugar, add half the tepid water and the corn oil, and mix well. Sieve the flour and add the contents of the packet of soup. Mix to a stiff dough, adding more, or all, of the tepid water to make a nice pliable mixture. Beat well till the dough leaves the sides of the bowl clean. Cover with a cloth and leave in a warm place till it doubles its size. Divide into small portions and shape into rolls. Leave to prove on a greased baking sheet 10–15 minutes. Bake at 425°F (Mark 7) for 12–15 minutes. To freeze, pack when cool in polythene bags.

Serve with cheese.

Bridge Rolls

1 lb flour
A pinch of salt
1 egg
2 oz lard
½ oz fresh yeast *or* ¼ oz dried yeast
2 tsps sugar
½ pint lukewarm water

Put the yeast and the sugar into the lukewarm water and allow to froth. Rub the lard into the flour and salt, then make a well in the centre and pour in the yeast mixture. Knead well. Cover with a cloth or plastic bag and leave in a warm place for about half-an-hour, then beat the egg and add it to the dough, mixing well in. Cover again and put back into a warm place to rise to double its original size.
Knead again and divide the dough into small pieces. Shape the pieces of dough into small oval shapes and place them on a well-greased baking sheet, putting them well apart to allow for rising. Cover again and leave to rise, then bake at 475°F (Mark 9) for about 10 minutes.

Potato Rolls

1 oz fresh yeast *or* ½ oz dried yeast
¼ cup of water
½ cup of hot mashed potatoes
¼ cup of oil or melted fat
¼ cup of sugar
1½ tsps salt
1 cup of hot milk
1 egg
4–4½ cups white flour
Use the same cup throughout.

Soften the yeast in warm water. Combine the potatoes, fat, sugar, salt and hot milk. Cool to lukewarm. Add yeast, now softened, and the egg. Stir in 2 cups of flour and beat well. Stir in the rest of the flour sufficient to make a nice soft dough. Knead on a lightly floured board until like silk (6–8 minutes). Place in a slightly greased bowl, turning the dough around once to grease all the surface. Cover and allow to stand till double in size (about 1 hour).

Punch down. Shape into a ball, then cover and allow to rest for a further 10 minutes. Shape into 24 rolls and place on the baking sheet which has been greased and lightly floured. Allow to rise again to almost double (about 1 hour). Bake at 400°F (Mark 6) for 10–12 minutes.

Yorkshire Teacakes

2 lb flour
4 oz butter
2 eggs
2 level tsps salt
1 level tsp sugar
1 pint of milk
$\frac{3}{4}$ oz fresh yeast *or* **$\frac{3}{8}$ oz dried yeast**

Melt the butter in the milk, allow to cool to lukewarm, then add with sugar to the yeast. Beat the eggs well and add them, together with the yeast mixture, to the flour and salt. Knead the dough well, then cover with a cloth or plastic bag, and leave in a warm place to double its original size. Knead the dough a second time and divide into 12 pieces. Shape these pieces into flat, round cakes, place them on a well-greased baking tray, cover and leave to rise again. Bake in a moderate oven 375°F (Mark 5) for approximately 30 minutes, but avoid letting them get too brown.

Sweet Buns

These sweet, fruity buns are a variation on the rolls—but do not expect to keep many in the tin. Here again, as with all small breads, they make ideal additions to the deep freeze.

Bannocks

1 lb flour
1 tsp salt
$\frac{1}{4}$ pint milk
2 oz lard or butter
$\frac{1}{2}$ oz fresh yeast *or* **$\frac{1}{4}$ oz dried yeast**
1 tsp sugar
$\frac{1}{4}$ pint tepid water
2 oz sugar
1 oz sultanas
1 oz currants
$\frac{1}{2}$ oz finely chopped peel

Sift the flour and salt into a warm mixing bowl, and leave to warm.

Heat the milk to lukewarm; add the lard and allow it to melt. Cool this liquid until tepid.

Cream the yeast with a teaspoon of sugar, and add the resulting liquid to the milk and lard mixture. Make a well in the middle of the flour and pour in the yeasty milk liquid; cover with some of the flour and cover the bowl with a clean cloth or large plastic bag and put in a warm place until bubbles appear on the surface.

Beat the flour and liquid together and add enough tepid water to make a soft dough. Knead well, then cover the bowl again and put back into the warm place to rise to double its original size.

Knead again, and work in the fruit and sugar. Form into two round flat cakes and put onto a greased baking sheet. Allow to rise for 20 minutes. Bake at 350°F (Mark 4) until golden brown (about 35 minutes) turning the loaves once.

Dissolve a little sugar in boiling water, and glaze the tops of the loaves. Return them to the oven for about two minutes to dry.

Cornish Yeast Buns

As made by Valerie Honey at Newquay Grammar School, 1940

8 oz flour
1 oz margarine
¼ tsp salt
1 oz sugar plus 1 tsp
1 oz currants
½ oz fresh yeast *or* ¼ oz dried yeast
¼ pint warm milk

Warm the mixing bowl and flour. Rub the fat into the warm flour; add the salt, 2 oz sugar and currants and mix well. Put the yeast in the warm milk and add the tsp of sugar; allow to froth. Make a well in the centre of the flour mixture and pour in the frothy liquid. Mix to a soft dough and knead well. Cover the bowl with a cloth or large plastic bag and leave to rise in a warm place for about an hour. Turn the dough onto a floured board, knead again, and shape into little buns. Cover again, and put to rise for a further 20 minutes. Bake on the top shelf of the oven at 425°F (Mark 7) for 20 minutes.

Betty's Sweet Yeast Buns

1 lb strong plain flour
1 tsp salt
2 oz sugar plus 1 tsp
A handful of dried mixed fruit
1 oz fresh yeast
1 tsp sugar

½ pint milk
2 oz chopped lard
1 medium egg

Place the flour, salt, 2 oz sugar and fruit to warm. Cream the yeast with the teaspoon of sugar. Beat the egg and add to the yeast mixture. Heat the milk—but do not boil—add the chopped lard and allow to melt into the milk. Cool to blood heat. Make a well in the flour mixture and mix well with a wooden spoon. Allow 2–2½ hours to rise, and beat again with a spoon. Shape into buns, allowing a further 30–40 minutes for a second rising. Bake at 425°F (Mark 7) for approximately 15 minutes.

Makes 16 buns or 4 teacake-size buns.

Currant Buns

8 oz flour
A pinch of salt
2 oz margarine
3 oz currants
1 egg
½ oz fresh yeast *or* ¼ oz dried yeast
⅛ pint (2 tbsps) tepid water
1 oz sugar
½ tsp mixed spice

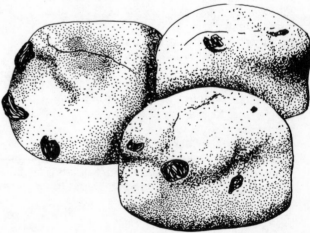

Put the yeast and the sugar in the tepid water. Mix the salt with the flour and rub in the margarine, then add the yeast mixture and knead well. Cover with a cloth or plastic bag and leave in a warm place to rise to double its original size. Knead again in the bowl and add the mixed spice and currants together with the beaten egg. Roll the dough with the hands into 10-12 balls on a lightly floured board, and place on a well-greased baking tray, leaving plenty of room between them to allow for rising. Cover again and leave in a warm place for about 10 minutes, then bake at 425°F (Mark 7) for 5 minutes, then reduce the heat to 375°F (Mark 5) for a further 5 minutes.

While the buns are still hot, brush them with a little melted sugar to glaze them. This adds the finishing touch to a delicious, light bun.

Tips

- While the dough is rising the first time, beat the egg and soak the currants and spice in the egg until required—this saves time in the next stage.
- Use a *very* little flour on the fingers when kneading in the egg mixture, if need be.

Orkney Cinnamon Buns

from Christine Muir

1 lb plain or strong flour
$\frac{1}{2}$ tsp salt
12 tbsps warm milk
1 egg, beaten
2 oz melted butter or margarine
1 tsp sugar
2 level tsps dried yeast
Butter or margarine, brown sugar
  and cinnamon to taste

Sprinkle the yeast on to the milk and sugar, add 2 tbsps of flour and beat all well. Leave to rise (20 minutes). Pour into the warm flour, add the butter or margarine and egg. Knead well (it will leave the bowl clean almost at once). Let it rise for 1 hour.

Spread the base of a square tin, 8 in. × 8 in. or similar, thickly with margarine or butter, brown sugar and cinnamon. Roll out the dough, spread with margarine or butter, brown sugar and cinnamon, roll up like a swiss roll, cut into slices and place in the tin side by side. Leave for 20 minutes to rise, then bake at 400°F (Mark 6) for about 20 minutes and turn out. The bottom of the buns becomes the top.

In St. David's, Pembs., the smallest city in the UK, there is only one baker—David Evans, known as Dai Crust. His bread is so delicious that visitors to the city take home quantities of it.

When Prince Charles' Investiture as Prince of Wales took place, Dai Crust was asked to bake the rolls to be served at the County Celebration Luncheon where, of course, His Royal Highness was to be Guest of Honour.

The Prince, it seems, had a second helping, and from that day to this, Dai Crust has been known as Dai Upper Crust!

Breads International, Love Breads and Celebration Breads

'To be important is nice—but to be nice is more important'

Old Jewish saying

Bread is one of the oldest known foods, as has been said, since in one form or other it is basic to most diets, world-wide.

In exchanging recipes, a sort of friendship springs up which is possibly closer and deeper than most because the cooks can then picture each other in their differing homes and environments, which forges a lasting bond.

So cooks of the world—generally housewives—can play their own important part in uniting the nations by ignoring any ethnic barriers and getting down to the nitty-gritty of swapping recipes and making each other's dishes.

Many a neighbourhood has suddenly sprung into communal life after one or two brave souls have met and talked about food. After all, there is nothing more flattering than to have one's cooking efforts admired to the extent of being asked for the recipe.

Love Breads come into this category of neighbourliness by reason of the motive behind baking them. A Love Bread is a sample of one's best bread, taken when visiting a home celebrating an engagement, golden wedding, return of a traveller, or where there is sickness in the house when the housewife may be too busy to bake or even to shop. In this area of West Wales if there is a funeral in the locality many good souls—usually also the best cooks—take samples of their cooking as contributions to feeding the many relatives, friends and neighbours who flock to the house after the service.

Taking a loaf of bread in the hand is the key which opens many a door at which we might otherwise be too diffident to knock.

Colrain Rye Bread

From Gail Hatch

'This is my favourite bread to take when we go visiting our friends in Colrain, Massachusetts. It's always enjoyed and appreciated—good with lots of butter and good conversation,' says Gail.

2 level tbsps dried yeast
7 fluid oz hot water
⅔ cup molasses (black treacle)
1 tbsp carraway seeds
1 tbsp dried grated orange rind *or*
    2–3 tbsps fresh orange rind
Yellow corn meal, or wholewheat
    flour—enough to dust the baking
    tins
1¼ lb rye flour
1 lb wholewheat flour
12 oz white flour
½ pint warm water
2 tbsps butter
1½ tbsps salt
1 tbsp anise seeds

Dissolve the yeast in the warm water. In a large bowl melt the butter in the hot water and add the other ingredients apart from the flour and finally the yeast mixture. Then sift together the rye, wholewheat and white flours and gradually add them to the liquid, stirring well to make a stiff dough. Knead the dough on a floured board until smooth and elastic. Place it in a greased bowl, cover with a cloth and leave to rise until double—about 1½–2 hours. Punch down; divide into 2 round loaves and place on a baking sheet, dusted with cornmeal. Cover and leave to rise until almost double. Then bake at 350°F (Mark 4) for 45–50 minutes.

Guatemalan Hunza Bread— 'Chapattis'

These take so little time to make and taste like a wheat field! The Hunzas are the race that live in a remarkable state of health— some have lived to be 145 years old.

For 2 people:
4 oz freshly ground wholewheat
  flour
¼ tsp salt
6 tbsps butter or margarine
1 generous fluid oz water

Mix the fat into the flour and salt. Add the water, knead, and leave for 30 minutes.

Divide into small balls, flatten with the hands and roll out to small flat rounds— about 3 in. in diameter. Cook on a greased griddle on each side for a few minutes.

Eat immediately with butter.

Pooree Indian Bread

1 lb wholewheat flour, sifted
¼ tsp salt
½ pint oil for frying

4 oz butter
Milk to mix

Mix the flour, salt and butter and just enough milk to make a firm, dry dough. Divide into small balls, about the size of a hen's egg.

Roll out the dough into shapes about 4–5 inches in diameter and ⅛ in. thick. Heat the oil and deep fry until golden brown.

Drain and serve.

Tangy German Rye Bread

The lemon peel in this delightful bread gives it its own unique flavour.

½ oz dried yeast
2 tbsps butter
2 tbsps freshly grated lemon rind
1 tbsp salt
⅔ cup currants
1 lb rye flour
1 cup wheatgerm
1 lb wholewheat flour
1 cup gluten flour (*or* white if gluten
  is not available)
⅛ pint lukewarm water
1 tbsp caraway seeds
2 tbsps molasses
1 pint milk

Dissolve the yeast in the warm water. Put the butter, caraway seeds, lemon peel, salt, molasses and currants in a large mixing bowl. Scald the milk and add it to the mixture. When the butter has melted and the milk cooled, stir in the yeast, then the rye flour and half the wholewheat. Beat vigorously, preferably in an electric mixer, until smooth. Add the wheatgerm and gluten flour and beat until stiff.

Pour out some of the remaining whole-wheat flour on a large board. Turn the dough onto it and dust with flour, kneading until it is smooth and elastic. Leave to rise, covered with a cloth, in a large buttered bowl, until doubled in size. Punch down and form into 2 loaves. Place seam-down on a lightly floured baking sheet—cover and leave to rise till double. Brush with cold water and bake for 50 minutes at 375°F (Mark 5).

Cranberry Thanksgiving Bread

A good bread for little ones as they can help chop the cranberries and nuts

8 oz flour
1½ tsps baking powder
½ tsp baking soda
1 egg, beaten
3–4 fluid oz orange juice
¾ cup chopped walnuts or pecans
  (optional)
1½ cups fresh or frozen whole
  cranberries, chopped in half
8 oz sugar
1 tsp salt
1 oz margarine or butter
1 tsp grated orange peel
1 cup light raisins

Sift flour, baking powder, salt and baking soda into a large bowl. Cut in the margarine until mixture is crumbly. Add the egg, orange peel, and orange juice all at once. Stir until the mixture is just evenly moist. Fold in the raisins, cranberries and nuts.

Spoon into a greased and floured 9 × 5 × 3 inch tin and bake at 350°F (Mark 4) for an hour. If the middle is still moist when tested, let it bake for 5–10 minutes more. Leave to cool slightly, remove from the tin and cool on a wire rack.

If desired, you may substitute cranberries for raisins to have an all-cranberry bread.

Marmalade Bread

5 good tbsps marmalade
3 oz melted Spry (or similar)
12 oz plain flour
7½ fluid oz orange juice
3 tsps baking powder
1 tsp bicarbonate of soda
1 egg
1 cup chopped nuts
1 tsp salt

Mix all the dry ingredients together. Keeping back 1 tbsp of marmalade, mix the rest with all the other remaining ingredients, except the nuts. Add to the flour mixture and stir until moistened.

Fold in the nuts, then turn into the usual loaf tin, well greased. Bake for 60 minutes at 350°F (Mark 4).

When done, turn onto a baking sheet, spread the top with the remaining marmalade and return to the oven to cook for one minute more.

Brioches

From France

14 oz plain white flour
2 tbsps warm water
1 oz fresh yeast *or* ½ oz dried yeast
1 tbsp sugar
4 oz melted butter or margarine
3 large eggs
1 tsp salt

Into a smallish bowl put the warm water, the yeast and about 4 oz of the flour. Mix to form a ball. Slash with a sharp knife and stand the bowl in a larger bowl filled with warm water. Leave covered with a cloth, until the dough has doubled in size.

Meanwhile, break the eggs into the remaining flour and mix well. Beat thoroughly. Next add the melted fat, salt and sugar and beat again for 5 minutes. Take the yeast and flour mixture from the bowl, add it to the rest and mix. When well blended, stand aside in a warm place for about 5–6 hours until the dough has doubled in size, remembering first to cover the basin with a cloth to keep out draughts. Then knead the dough and set it aside (covered again) in a cool place overnight.

Next day, butter a rounded mould, place the dough in it and leave to rest for 30 mins. Finally, cook at 425°–450°F (Mark 7–8) for 35 minutes, protecting the top with foil or buttered paper to prevent burning.

Olive's Caerfarchell Teacakes

3 lb plain flour
3 eggs
3 tsps sugar
1½ pints milk or milk-and-water
6 oz margarine
3 oz fresh yeast
1 tsp salt

Put the flour and salt in a bowl. Place the yeast and sugar in a basin and leave until it is liquid. Put the margarine and milk in a saucepan, warm to blood heat, then whisk the eggs and when the yeast is ready put all the ingredients into the flour and mix with a fork. After mixing, sprinkle some flour on top, cover with a warm, damp cloth, and put in a warm place to rise. After it has risen, knead and roll out and cut into rounds, put on tins and again leave to double in size. Bake at 425–450°F (Mark 7–8) for 10–15 minutes, until golden brown.

Olive is a very good cook and a generous soul who has a wonderful reputation on account of her teacakes. She rarely makes them just for her family, but can always be relied on to help out when there is a party or a funeral.

What Went Wrong?

Sometimes even the best of cooks has a failure. The results are seldom so awful as to be inedible, but if you want to aim for perfection next time, you may find the following hints helpful.

Oven Scones

1. *My scones were heavy and didn't rise much.*
   This can be caused by:
   (a) not enough raising agent,
   (b) not enough liquid,
   (c) too much heavy handling, especially of the scraps,
   (d) the scones were kept waiting to go in the oven, or
   (e) the temperature of the oven was too low—or the scones were put too low in the oven.

2. *My scones 'ran' all over the place.*
   If your scones lose shape like this it usually means that either too much liquid or too much raising agent was used. Also, if you are of a generous nature and over-grease your tin, the scones tend to skid when the fat gets hot in the oven. This spreads them too much and they lose shape.

3. *My scones looked like the Leaning Tower of Pisa!*
   If your scones go lopsided or rise unevenly, this may be caused by one of the following:
   (a) The mixture wasn't kneaded sufficiently—but remember, it must be done oh, so lightly!
   (b) When cutting the dough the cutter wasn't floured often enough.
   (c) When transferring the uncooked scones to the tin, they weren't handled carefully enough.
   (d) The dough wasn't rolled out evenly.

4. *What made my scones have burnt bottoms but underdone tops and middles?*
   Get to know your type of cooker. If the heat comes from all round—as in solid fuel ones—a tray right across the oven works alright. But with gas, for instance, it is possible for too large a tray or tin to block the heat and stop it circulating properly; the heat then reaches only the bottom of the tin and doesn't rise sufficiently to the top of the oven.

Griddle Scones

1. *My scones looked cooked but they were raw inside.*
   Test the heat of the griddle before you start cooking (see p. 27)—if it is too hot the scones will be quickly browned but will not have time to cook inside.

2. *My scones 'ran' all over the place.*
   The batter was too thin; just add a little more flour and beat it in well. It should only just pour from the spoon—only a little thinner than mayonnaise.

3. *The scones stuck to the griddle.*
   Though you must take care not to over-grease the griddle, sufficient grease must be rubbed in to prevent sticking. Try rubbing the griddle with a greasy cloth after cooking is finished each time. If it gets very bitty, rub dry salt on to clean it and rub off with a soft tissue.
   A good tip for greasing it is to tie a bit of hard fat such as suet in a bag of muslin and keep that for the purpose. Afterwards, store in a plastic bag—muslin and all—in the freezing compartment of your refrigerator.

Yeasted Breads

1. *My dough was heavy and 'close' with hardly any increase in bulk after the first rising*
The yeast was killed because the liquid you added was too hot—only *tepid* water, please!

2. *Why didn't the dough increase with the second rising?*
The dough was put to rise in too hot a place. Better cooler than too hot—it may take a little longer but it saves waste and disappointment.

3. *Why did the dough rise only very slowly?*
There are two likely causes for this:
(a) The yeast was stale or too cold; stale yeast also smells unpleasant. Yeast that has been stored in the fridge or deep freeze needs time, *at room temperature,* to warm up. Don't hurry it—you'll kill it.
(b) The dough wasn't wet enough. Try kneading in, a little at a time, a small cup of tepid water. You may save the day!

4. *My loaf was well risen but the top was all wrinkled and there was a heavy layer just below the surface.*
There could be two reasons for this:
(a) The dough was left to prove for too long. What happens is that the gluten—the sticky agent in the flour—becomes over-stretched and can no longer 'hold it all together' so the dough collapses.
(b) The oven wasn't hot enough to start with.

5. *My bread was lovely to look at from the outside, but it had great holes in it.*
Again, there are two possible causes:
(a) The oven wasn't hot enough to start with.
(b) You didn't knead for long enough after the first rising; this results in the gas and yeast being unevenly distributed. The 'quick' brown breads are the ones to watch in this regard—if you possibly can, it does pay to spend a minute or two kneading the dough just before you put it in the tins.

6. *My bread was badly risen and had a nasty close texture.*
Check your methods and make sure that:
(a) the dough has long enough to 'prove' or rise, and
(b) sufficient liquid is added—a 'dry' dough, you see, feels more like pastry to handle whereas bread dough, at its best, is like silk or satin to handle and is as smooth (if you'll pardon the expression) as a baby's bottom. You'll soon recognise this texture when you achieve it—and you'll soon do that!

7. *When I made dinner rolls, they cracked around the base and yet the bottoms were heavy.*
If rolls are put to rise in too warm a place the yeast is killed. This causes a skin to form over the roll which then cracks in the oven.

8. *The bread I made tasted sour and nasty.*
There are three possible causes:
(a) The yeast was stale.
(b) Too much yeast was used.
(c) The rising and proving process was too slow and so acid developed.

Index